CREATED TO NETWORK

STRATEGIC NETWORKING FOR PURPOSE-DRIVEN NETWORKERS

KISHA L. ALLEN

Copyright 2016 © by Kisha L. Allen (Version 2)

ALL RIGHTS RESERVED, no part of this book may be reproduced in any form without permission or written consent from the writer. Media, reviewers, bloggers, etc. may quote passages.

GROUP DISCOUNTS & BULK PURCHASES:

Universities, Colleges, Corporations, and Other Professional Organizations: Submit all speaker booking requests, information, special discount or bulk purchase requests to admin@movebeyondmotivation.com or 972.926.3124.

Website: www.movebeyondmotivation.com

DISCLAIMER

Please be advised that if legal, medical or psychological help is needed, please seek the assistance and guidance of a professional or expert in these fields. Use of this book constitutes acceptance of the "No Liability" policy.

Design by Cover Creators
Edited by Tony Guerra

Manufactured in the United States of America

ISBN-13: 978-0692706916
ISBN-10: 0692706917

ACKNOWLEDGEMENTS

All honor, praise and glory be to God. This book is dedicated to my family...my husband Cameron, my daughter Shae, my mother Kimberley and my sisters Cynthia, LaToya and LaKrisha for always supporting me. And to every person along the way that has poured into and encouraged me, THANK YOU, THANK YOU, THANK YOU!

YOU ARE HERE FOR A REASON

You are who you are for a reason.
You're part of an intricate plan.
You're a precious and perfect unique design,
Called God's special woman or man.

You look like you look for a reason.
Our God made no mistake.
He knit you together within the womb,
You're just what he wanted to make.

The parents you had were the ones he chose,
And no matter how you may feel,
They were custom designed with God's plan in mind,
And they bear the Master's seal.

No, that trauma you faced was not easy.
And God wept that it hurt you so;
But it was allowed to shape your heart
So that into his likeness you'd grow.

You are who you are for a reason,
You've been formed by the Master's rod.
You are who you are, beloved,
Because there is a God!

-- Russell Kelfer

CONTENTS
Your Guide to Purpose Driven Networking

You Are Here for a Reason	4
Introduction	7
1 Created to Network	11
2 Cultivating a Harvester's Mindset	21
3 Establishing Trust & Credibility	25
Protect Yourself and Your Network	29

BEFORE THE EVENT

Equipment	34
4 Create Your Purpose Brand	35
Step 1: Who am I?	38
Step 2: How Do Others See You?	43
Step 3: Identify Your Target Customer	47
Step 4: Establish Your Value Proposition	57

Step 5: Craft An Award Winning Pitch (AWP)   61
Step 6: Complete Your Brand Profile Summary   63
Pre-Networking Purpose Brand Checklist   64

5 Networking Is Every Where: Identifying Opportunities   71
Leveraging Your Existing Network   73
Networking Online   81
Content Creation Ideas   103
Build Your Weekly Networking Strategy   119

DURING THE EVENT

6 BE You, DO You and HAVE FUN DOING IT!   117
Strategies for Effective Networking   121
Strategies for Delivering an Award-Winning Pitch   124
Graceful Exit Strategies   125

AFTER THE EVENT

7 The Fortunes in the Follow-up   129
The 5 Step Networking Follow-Up Process   133

Spread the Word   138

INTRODUCTION

"We do not segment our lives, giving some time to God, some to our business or schooling, while keeping parts to ourselves. The idea is to live all of our lives in the presence of God, under the authority of God, and for the honor and glory of God. That is what the Christian life is all about." ~ R.C. Sproul

For he chose us in him before the creation of the world to be holy and blameless in his sight. In love. (Ephesians 1:4 NIV)

For nine years, I had the opportunity to work at a local Chamber of Commerce, where I fell in love with networking. I realized that networking and connecting with others fueled me. During this time, I heard many networking horror stories, but I was also exposed to many success stories. As a result of my networking experiences, I was able to perfect the way I networked. There were many days that I would attend networking events and find myself walking through a crowd of people or standing off in a corner, smiling from ear to ear, enjoying the energy of the room. It was in these moments that I became aware of the true rhythm of networking, it's importance, and what it meant to connect. I enjoyed watching people interact, the laughter, the deep conversations, and the opportunities being shared. Every time, I experience true networking, I am reminded that it's what we we're created to do. Connection is necessary and its food for the soul. My energy is a direct result of what happens when you stay connected and remain in the flow of life. The flow is disrupted when you aren't networking and connecting with others. The more you interact with others, you'll find that your energy is increased as you laugh, smile, encourage each other, or share information and resources. I 've learned that it's not about who you know or who knows you, it's truly about relationship and trust. The truth is, I don't care who knows you, if they don't trust you, it's pointless.

The time that I spent at the Chamber taught me many valuable lessons about networking and as a result, my days have been filled with making true, authentic connections. We've tried to formalize networking down to a science, further frustrating ourselves, making the process harder than it should be. Networking shouldn't be hard. I've learned that effective networkers, must be open, receiving each connection for the beauty and value it is designed to bring; however, it shows up. It's not about the money, new business, or status, while these are the results that you will experience. It's always about what you can give and pour into each person you encounter. A true networker recognizes that they are a vessel, carrying a gift that they are called to share with others. These gifts open seemingly magical doors for business opportunities, information, resources and referrals.

On your journey to destiny, you're going to need help and that help is surrounding you and always right there when you need it. If you're truly ready to live on purpose, you will need resources for maximum impact. Networking gives you access to these resources and if you play your cards right, you'll find that these resources are always right on time. Everything you need is in your network and what you don't have is available through networking. I have seen and experienced the power of networking in my own life and that's why this book exists.

You are the key to shifting the world around you and unlocking the divine potential in every person you encounter.

Who is this book for?

This book is for every purpose-driven individual, who is ready to access the promises that have been spoken over their lives. Whether you're a man, woman or child, college student, professional, mom, dad or business owner, this book is for you. Understand that you we're created to network, so networking shouldn't be hard or frustrating. This book will help you break down barriers that have hindered your growth, so that you can access everything in life that was meant for you. I challenge you to become more conscious as you network, delivering an experience that blows the mind of every person you encounter. Approach every connection, seeking the opportunity to be a resource by serving them with your skills, gifts, talents and expertise. As you serve others, you will grow personally, spiritually, professionally and mentally.

"Everything you want in life is a relationship away."
~ Idowu Koyenikan

1
CREATED TO NETWORK

Thought is the wind, knowledge the sail, and mankind the vessel.
~ Augustus Hare

7 But we have this treasure in earthen vessels, so that the surpassing greatness of the power will be of God and not from ourselves; **8** we are afflicted in every way, but not crushed; perplexed, but not despairing; **9** persecuted, but not forsaken; struck down, but not destroyed; **10** always carrying about in the body the dying of Jesus, so that the life of Jesus also may be manifested in our body. (2 Corinthians 4:7-9)

WE ARE ALL VESSELS

Before we dive into the topic of networking and making connections, it is very important that you understand and recognize that you are a vessel, carrying the essence of God within you. Your body is the vessel that is being used to transport God's love and gifts, here on earth to meet the needs of everyone you are called to serve. Because you are his vessel, you must move about the earth networking, sharing what he has given you with the world.

In Genesis 41:15-16, when Joseph was called to interpret Pharaoh's dream, he told Pharaoh that God would provide the interpretation; Joseph made it very clear that he was only a vessel, the mouth piece that God would use. I know you've heard many times that it's not about you, but on some level, it is – it's about your life and what you choose to do with it. Someone is waiting for you to show up, somewhere, so that they can receive what you are carrying for them. We need each other more than we'll ever know or understand. In Genesis 2:18, when God created Eve for Adam, he said, that it isn't good for man to be alone. Because the truth is, life is too hard to go at it alone. We all need help, no matter how strong, smart, cute or funny you are. We were not created to take this journey of life alone. Again, this is why we all must network and connect with those we were created to serve. We desperately need each other to live, thrive and survive.

As a purpose-driven individual, you must value people and take ownership of the relationships you are responsible for, honoring each person that you encounter. You must see every human being as someone special, God's precious son or daughter and not an opportunity or dollar sign. Every person you encounter is a vessel of God, carrying precious cargo (God's love and gifts). We should look at each other and see a sign that says handle with care, fragile or DO NOT BREAK. When you encounter someone, your heart should smile first and that same smile should show up on your face as an outward expression of what's going on inside. I challenge you to greet every person you meet with a smile and hello, especially if you are within arm's reach. You never know who a person really is and what they have access to, so treat everyone respectfully, despite their circumstances and what they look like.

We we're created to pour out of ourselves, to give and share, so an exchange must happen. If you are a purpose-driven individual, you must take ownership of the fact that you are a vessel and networking is your lifestyle. It emanates from your core and being. As a vessel you are transporting something to an intended person or destination. You we're designed with something and someone specific in mind. Keep in mind that a vessel with a hole, can't be filled with anything because it will run out. To avoid this issue, you must always be working on yourself to make sure that all holes and brokenness are being repaired as they arise. Also keep in mind that vessels are designed to carry different things. A vessel designed to carry cars or large cargo, can't be used to carry something small. It would be a waste of time and space. When you understand this, you also understand that what you have isn't for everyone, so stop trying to sell everyone. Rejection isn't a bad thing, it keeps you from wasting valuable time, energy and effort. When you experience rejection. Learn to dust yourself off and keep moving; carry your products,

When someone rejects what you're offering, they aren't rejecting you, what they are saying is, "What you have isn't meant for me."

services and gifts to those that they were created for, so that it will bring them value." As a vessel carrying precious cargo, you are hired to get it to the correct person, on time and in good condition. This is why you must network with your target market or customer, which you will identify in Chapter 4.

net·work·ing

the exchange of information or services among individuals, groups, or institutions; *specifically*: the cultivation of productive relationships for employment or business

con·nect·ing

to join two or more things together: to think of (something or someone) as being related to or involved with another person, thing, event, or idea

WHY DO WE NETWORK?

Networking is more than just an activity to increase sales; it's an exchange of information or services among individuals, groups or institutions; specifically, the cultivation of productive relationships for employment or business. As you are networking, please keep in mind that selling isn't bad, because networking, done right, accelerates sales. You're always selling something, whether you know it or not. They key is, you want to sell to the right people, at the right time, giving them an experience they'll never forget.

Networking is not just a necessity to get what you want in life and business, but a responsibility that you must take ownership of as a means to fulfill your purpose in life.

For networking to occur, you must be growing and caring for those you're in relationship with, giving and practicing the art of reciprocity, ultimately developing productive relationships that yield a return. When living in and on purpose, the question is no longer, "What's in it for me", but "How can I serve you?" Of course, as with anything, you must establish boundaries to avoid being misused.

As a purpose-driven networker, you give as much, if not more than you take. It's about planting, nurturing and watering the right seeds. Networking is critical for the growth and sustainability of our relationships, communities and businesses. We've made networking into a bad word and we tell people to stop networking and start connecting. I've said it myself, until I realized that the issue isn't networking, it's you and me. Networking and connecting work hand in hand. It's what drives growth in our communities, businesses and economy, so we must learn to respect, honor and reverence it, as we once did. You must understand that networking requires you to be conscious, open and aware, so that the opportunity to connect isn't missed, because true networking only happens after a connection is made. The connection is the key to opening the door to what you have need of; sales, money, referrals and everything else will come, if you handle your true assignment of connecting first.

Networking is art in its purest form. If we don't honor its value, we're going to miss out on its extraordinary power and results. This artistic form of expression allows you the opportunity to use your gifts freely in the world to create opportunities and facilitate change. It is through networking that you are able to generate game-changing partnerships and movements that have impact. Without networking Martin Luther King wouldn't have been able to spark a movement that shifted a nation. We are living the results of what pure, authentic networking can produce. Most of the elected officials that currently hold seats and the fortune 500 companies that exist to date are the product of good, old fashioned, grass roots networking and door-to-door sales – building relationships and customers one-by-one.

Bottom line, networking helps you access the career you desire, find a workout partner, connect with a friend, find a credible plumber, buy your dream house or sell your company's products and services. Whatever you need in your life, business, or career, you can access it through networking. Networking isn't just about attending tons of events, collecting cards, making sales, meeting 1,000 people or having 100,000 social media followers, it's about true, authentic connections that become a vehicle for exchange. It's bigger than likes and shares, it's about connecting, engaging and continuously interacting, ultimately serving and meeting each other's needs with our skills, services, gifts and talents.

Everything you have need of is in your network.

As a disciple of Christ, networking correlates with what we were created to do. As purpose driven people, our assignment (if we look at Jesus as our example) is to love, give and serve each other. When you understand that you were created to network, you show up understanding that you are called to be a God experience, here on earth, connecting, giving, serving, sharing and operating in your gifts.

When you find yourself struggling or in need of something, give someone else what you have need of to ignite the flow of provision in your life.

As you connect, network, and serve the world, everything that you have need of in life will seemingly show up, right on time. Zig Ziglar said it best, "You can have everything you want in life, if you will just help enough other people get what they want."

With all of this being said, networking and connecting isn't as hard as most people make it. To be an effective networker, you must release ego and selfish motives, allowing it to flow naturally out of your core and the authenticity of your being. Pursuing networking from this standpoint means that you intentionally become more strategic, listening and watching for divine clues (Proverbs 3:6). You aren't so focused on a sale that you miss bigger opportunities. The truth is, when it comes to cultivating and creating productive relationships, you must be strategic because every person has different needs. You must be mindful of this because your network is a huge investment that provides so much value. As with any investment, you must put something in to get a return, understanding that there will be highs and lows. Don't spend all of your time focused on the lows. Don't ever allow frustration and disappointment to discourage you. When managing any investment, you understand that it decreases when you make a withdrawal. The same rule holds true with networking and relationships. I call it the *Relationship Investment Strategy*. This strategy simply indicates that you never take more than you're willing to give back and if you make a withdrawal, you will reinvest at least what you withdrew, if not more. This reinvestment could be financial, knowledge-based, sharing your gifts, or providing a product or service to someone. When you understand that you were created to network, you recognize that networking is the vehicle you use to connect to the assignments and opportunities you are called to. To do this and have this be your experience, you must become consciously aware, expanding yourself to receive every opportunity, outside of the sale, with the sale being the icing on the cake.

"Your network is priceless. It is filled with everything you need to be successful in life. Each person in your network is a vessel carrying something that you need, so it's in your best interest to handle it and everyone in it with care."

NETWORKING GRANTS YOU ACCESS

(1) Access to everything you need to be successful in your life, business and relationships.

(2) Access to inspiration, motivation and encouragement. Through networking you not only receive encouragement, but you can also

encourage others. As you encourage others, you'll find yourself encouraged. Always remember, encouragement is free, transferable, positive energy that brightens any space.

(3) Access to career, business and volunteer opportunities, not only for you, but for your family, children, friends and other connections.

(4) Access to resources, support, assistance, information, training and experiences that can ultimately help you learn and grow. This information can be for professional or personal purposes. This is a great way to identify and strengthen your authentic gifts, talents and skills. The more you use them, the stronger they become. Whatever you need, if you don't know anyone, someone in your network does.

(5) Access to advice and valuable feedback – survey your customers/ network when you need advice or feedback on projects or major decisions. Networking with the right people will cause you to have influence that will prove invaluable when you need support.

(6) Access to money and resources to start and finance a business.

(7) Access to friendships, strategic partnerships, customers, suppliers, vendors, employers, referrals and internships can all be found when networking. You can even meet your future spouse.

(8) And what we all look forwarded to, access to more sales and increased income/ revenue.

DECLARATIONS FOR PURPOSE-DRIVEN NETWORKERS

(1) I am love. Love is my standard. It's at the core of who I am.

(2) I am conscious, wide awake, paying close attention to the flow, heart beat and energy I am surrounded by daily, flowing in its rhythm.

Because of this awareness, I see and hear opportunities that may have otherwise been missed.

(3) I am patient. I understand that it takes time to cultivate productive relationships that grant me influence.

(4) I am confident being myself. I know who I am and understand my purpose. I know exactly what I have been called to do. I deliver memorable experiences that glorify God. I follow-up and deliver on every promise made with excellence.

(5) I am happy and excited about life because I live all out.

(6) I am energetic. My energy is contagious, lighting up the room wherever I go. I am always mindful of how I show up in the world.

(7) I am self-less and humble. I overcome rejection with a smile on my face, never taking it personally.

(8) I am a connecter. Every day I seek to build genuine relationships. I honor every person I meet. It's not about titles, whose important and who's not. I add value to the lives of others by strategically connecting them to people, information and resources.

(9) When I network, I notice those that are standing alone and seek to engage them. I see every person as God sees them, so I greet them with a smile.

(10) I am an interviewer. I am a good communicator and great listener. I ask the right questions and my focus is on connecting, listening and seeking opportunities to serve and provide value.

(11) I understand that networking starts with a simple hello and a smile, so every day I make a conscious decision to greet every person I pass or am standing near.

"Love of God and people will pave roads where there were once none." ~ Shannon L. Alder

2 CULTIVATING A HARVESTERS' MINDSET

Read Matthew 13:3-9 and Mark 4:3-8

I have found that the more I honored others, the more they honored me and the more fulfilling my career became. In the business arena, I have been surrounded by people with awesome skills. The difference between good and great is determined by the mindset you choose to bring to work. The concept of honor should be part of that mindset.
~ Douglas Conant

Change your thinking, change your expectations and ultimately change your experiences.

You must understand that your thoughts are the root of everything you are and will produce in your life, businesses and relationships. You must also understand that thought is the origin of wealth, success, happiness, inventions, and achievements or the opposite. If you are struggling with lack, negativity sadness or anger, check your thoughts. Your thoughts manifest in your life; good, bad or indifferent, your life is the by-product of your thoughts. With that being said, if you have negative thoughts in relation to networking, what you believe is what you will experience.

If you always think, "This is a waste of time," guess what it is. If you constantly focus on how much you hate it or that the people are not friendly, guess what, these will be your experiences. If you constantly think your networking efforts don't produce results, guess what they won't. Change your thinking, change your expectations and ultimately change your experiences.

Purpose-driven networkers understand that to truly be a vessel, you must have a *Harvesters' Mindset*, operating in patience and understanding that all seeds must be strategically planted, nurtured, fed and watered to grow. This same concept holds true when it comes to networking. Harvesters' are always thinking about cultivation and growth. They always test and prepare the soil before planting anything to ensure that it's good ground for planting. You must learn to do the same when networking and making connections, as a means of identifying and connecting with those that you are called to. You must fully understand the importance of planting your seeds in the right soil and in the right season, if you expect to reap a harvest. Developing a harvesters' mindset is critical for your success. If you don't get it, you will find yourself scattering seeds all over the place, ultimately ending up with seeds that have fallen by the wayside to be eaten by birds. The same thing happens many times as you network. Most people run all over town networking, trying to sell everybody, yielding little or no results. This is why you can't be so quick sell. When networking, you should first assess the needs of the person you're connecting with, asking the right questions, paying close attention to their words and actions as means of gauging whether or not you should invest your time, energy or effort. You are not called to serve everyone. If a seed is properly planted, nurtured and cared for, it will produce a plenteous harvest, yielding more than enough for you and everyone you're connected to.

Transitioning from a seedling to a field full of crops is a long drawn out process that takes time. When approaching networking with a harvesters' mindset, you understand that the process of cultivating leads, prospects, referrals and new business opportunities will take time, but when they are ripe, they will create the results you desire. You must nurture and diligently tend to the seeds in your network to strengthen your relationships. This is why you must follow-up often and keep your connections engaged by meeting their needs as they arise and providing them with quality content, products and services. A harvester also understands that not every seed will yield fruit and which crops must be managed with care. The same thing applies to your network. A harvester masters the art of recognizing the maturity of plant so it doesn't stay out in the fields too long. They are also skilled at quickly harvesting plants once they have ripened, separating the consumable yields from the useless or unusable portions. Manage your relationships with care as not to damage them or burn bridges. Just as the harvester does, you must learn to release relationships that don't serve you or that are not in your best interest, even these relationships, should be managed respectfully and with care as you release them. Remember that some people come into your life for a reason, some a season, and some a lifetime (Whitney Garcia Williams)."

Harvesters' know that they cannot reap from what hasn't been sown, so they do everything with the end in mind, monitoring their crops regularly, living each day in expectation, awaiting the harvest from the seeds that we're planted. While you're cultivating your network and working to produce a harvest, you must keep yourself encouraged along the way, celebrating your accomplishments and practicing thankfulness and gratefulness. This is a critical component of cultivating a harvesters' mindset. As a harvester, you must learn to live in the flow, consciously awake, aware of everything going on in and around you. You must awake every day, allowing everything to happen authentically and naturally, moving about your day, expressing love everywhere you go.

What does this mean? Love is action, so as you're networking, you should be planting seeds of love, allowing love to orchestrate the intended outcome. This could be practicing patience, kindness, a smile, being a listening ear, greeting someone, serving them in your gift, sharing your energy, encouraging them or speaking life. Whatever your seed of love is, plant it in the right soil and watch it produce a harvest. Remember, networking starts with a simple hello.

Tip: When you rise each day, start your day with gratitude and thankfulness for yesterday's harvest. Then express gratitude and thankfulness for the people and opportunities that you will access today. Next, pray for divine connections; ask that your eyes, ears, heart and spirit be open to every assignment awaiting you today. After you have done this, start your day with a self-help audiobook or music that inspires you.

BELIEFS OF A HARVESTER

(1) I work on myself daily, preparing the ground of my soul, tilling the soil of my life.

(2) I plant seeds of love everywhere I go. I am committed to cultivating strong, healthy relationships, feeding, watering and growing them, so that they will yield a plenteous harvest.

(3) The seeds that I plant are an investment, so I invest wisely in healthy stock that yields a substantial return. Everything that I invest in daily will yield a profitable return for me and everyone I am connected to.

(4) I study and meditate regularly, listening for divine strategies, taking action, planting and moving in season to yield the fruit of my labor. I am patient, operating consciously, so I never miss divine connections or opportunities.

(5) I am a giver. I never take from where I am not willing to give back and I always give a portion of my harvest back to my community.

3 ESTABLISHING TRUST & CREDIBILITY

Show yourself in all respects to be a model of good works, and in your teaching show integrity and dignity. (Titus 2:7)

"It takes 20 years to build a reputation and five minutes to ruin it."
~ Warren Buffet

One of the saddest things that I have noticed in today's marketplace is a lack of ethics. As a result of people taking advantage of others, trust is at an all-time low, making it even harder to do business. Trust seems to be a foreign concept to most people and we wonder why it takes so much time to build relationships and access opportunities. You must be trustworthy, if you want to accomplish anything in life. Trust is the foundation of any great relationship and the key to establishing influence. As it grows, relationships are strengthened.

Trust is the gateway to opportunity.

I know without a doubt that people want to do business with those that they like and trust. This has been my experience.

This is why our networking efforts have to be focused on more than just making and closing a sale. Trust can't be established overnight, but it's necessary to open the door to bigger opportunities.

WAYS TO BUILD TRUST & CREDIBILITY – JUST BE!

Be what you want to see in the world!

(1) Be confident, but not arrogant and toot your horn a little. Let everyone know that you're capable of performing the task. Then do what you said you we're going to do.

(2) Be and show love. Treat others better than you want to be treated. Be fair, always give and share freely, expecting nothing in return.

(3) Be accessible. Everyone wants convenience. They want to know you'll be there when they need you.

(4) Be honest, vulnerable and transparent. Always tell the truth, even when it hurts and look people in the eye when you're talking to them. Don't lie. Don't take what's not yours or more than what you've earned or poured in. Be trustworthy and operate ethically.

(5) Be responsible. Accept responsibility when you mess up and come prepared with solutions to correct the issue. People trust those that own their mistakes.

(6) Be professional and present yourself accordingly. Provide polished marketing materials (business cards, brochures, pictures, website, etc.). Make sure that all of your marketing materials and social media channels are consistent, delivering the same brand message. Use a professional email as well, hotandbothered@yahoo.com isn't professional or trustworthy. If you can't afford a branded email at this time, simply use your name or your business name.

(7) Be a man or woman of excellence. Provide quality products and services. Deliver on your brand promise. Make sure that your customer service is exceptional as well. Set a standard for yourself and live your values. Recognize the difference between excellence and perfection. Perfection is an impossible standard to live by. (Philippians 4:8)

ex·cel·lence

the quality of being outstanding or extremely good

per·fect·tion

1: the condition, state, or quality of being free or as free as possible from all flaws or defects

2: the action or process of improving something until it is faultless or as faultless as possible.

(8) Be a negotiator. Create win, win situations for yourself and your network. Meet them half way and choose your battles wisely.

(9) Be a good communicator. Ask the right questions, listen, and pay close attention to their body language. Make the person you're interacting with feel like they are the most important person in the room by giving them your undivided attention. Make eye contact. Ask open-ended questions to get and keep them engaged.

(10) Be respectful. Aretha Franklin said it best R-E-S-P-E-C-T, find out what it means to me. Don't gossip or talk about people. One of the

biggest trust breakers is overhearing someone talking about you negatively. It's hard to overcome.

(11) Be referable and a referrer. Ask your network periodically for referrals, testimonials and endorsements, then share them. When someone trustworthy refers or endorses you, everyone that trusts them will trust you. Don't ask people you don't have a relationship with or that have no experience with you for referrals or testimonials. Refer others as well.

(12) Be a connector. Always add value to those in your network. You can do this by providing information, resources, connecting them to others, etc.

(13) Be consistent, stay connected. You must communicate and stay connected with your network, even when you don't "need" them. Don't just contact them when you need something. Follow-up, follow-up, follow-up, even after the sale.

(14) Be dependable. Follow-through on your promises, be consistent and committed to the process. Don't start what you can't and aren't willing to finish.

(15) Be a teacher, always learning and growing. Teach, mentor and coach, invest in others by sharing wisdom, information and knowledge. If people know that you genuinely want to see them grow and do better, they'll trust you.

PROTECT YOURSELF AND YOUR NETWORK

A few years ago, my daughter and I planted a garden, but we did so without learning how to truly garden. We purchased soil and seedlings, then we planted them. We watered and fed the plants and they grew, but we didn't protect them. As our tomatoes lined the ground, grub worms and bugs feasted on them, destroying our crops. Our garden was beautiful and full of delicious vegetables, but we weren't able to see all of the bad things that were lurking in the soil, hiding amongst our harvest. The same thing happens in networking. In today's social media driven world, we have thousands of contacts and now people can see exactly who we know. We have so many connections that many times we miss the networking grub worms when they creep in. Don't get me wrong, I truly believe that our networks are meant to be shared, but let's be honest, there are times, when you don't feel comfortable introducing someone to those that you are connected to or allowing them to use your name. While I'd like to believe that everyone that networks, does so with good intentions; however, this is not the case, so we can't speak of harvesters' without addressing the larvae and grub worms that will devour your harvest (connections), if you don't protect them. These are the people that always want you to introduce them, but they never introduce you to anyone. They are aggressive, shifty and sneaky. They continuously draw from your well (resources) to water their garden or eat from your harvest, never offering you anything in return. They wait for the work of your hands to yield a harvest, so that they can enjoy the fruit without the labor. They are manipulators and will suck the life out of you and your connections. They have very few boundaries and don't easily accept no for an answer. Because you value your network, you must protect them from network grub worms. This is why discernment and boundaries are extremely important when it comes to networking. You must be careful of referring or partnering with any and every one. It could cause significant damage to your reputation. This is also why making true connections and building relationships is critical. Only refer and partner with those you truly know, trust and have vetted. At the end of the day, if push comes to shove, TRUST YOUR GUT because if they will use you, nine times out of ten they will use those that you refer them to. Also keep in mind that you can't share everything with everybody.

ESTABLISHING NETWORKING BOUNDARIES

> **bound·a·ries**
>
> unofficial rules about what should not be done: limits that define acceptable behavior

All relationships should be reciprocal, never one sided. To avoid one sided relationships, you must always be clear on your boundaries, needs and expectations. To establish boundaries, you must be willing to tell the truth, whether that's to yourself or others. Enforcing boundaries can be difficult as it requires boldness and courage. At some point there will be someone who tries to cross them, so you must be ready to deal with it accordingly, even if it means losing a sale, partnership or business opportunity. Below are a few ideas to help you stop network grub worms and habitual boundary crossers in their tracks.

(1) Know your limits. Be clear on them up front. Don't allow them to continuously be crossed. Remember you teach people how to treat you; every time you allow someone to get out of line, without saying anything, you are saying that it's okay.

(2) Listen to your gut/ feelings. If it doesn't feel right, more than likely, it's not. TRUST YOUR GUT!

(3) Avoid toxic influences and negativity when possible. Try to express yourself positively, even in negative situations. Focus on being positive and you will attract positive energy and people. Learn to release

negative people and relationships. Work through the issue, so that it doesn't continuously show up in your life and business.

(4) Be direct and courageous, don't beat around the bush. Learn to say NO! Say what you mean and mean what you say. Own your NO. Give yourself permission to say no. Every opportunity isn't a good opportunity. You don't always have to explain yourself. A simple no, I apologize, but I'm not interested will suffice.

(5) Establish strategic partnerships and affiliate or referral programs. Develop a contract and guidelines for each. Shifty and manipulative people tend to shy away from contracts and commitments. If all else fails and you just absolutely can't or don't want to deal with someone, call them after hours and leave them a voicemail or send them an email. In addition, you must make it a habit to establish contracts, even with friends and family members, to ensure that boundaries and expectations are clear, so that there's very little room for miscommunication and offense.

(6) If saying no is hard, blame it on your values, vision, goals needs, wants, or business practices. Know what these are and outline them. Once you have identified these things, you can govern yourself by them and when someone or something doesn't align with them, it's easier to tell them no. Here are a few ways to say NO to someone that wants access to your network or that wants to partner.

Example 1: "I value my partners and those within my network, so I actually have a referral fee or affiliate program for strategic partners. If you're interested in this, I can send you more information."

And for those that say they are interested in partnering, but you don't want to work with them you can say,

Example 2: "I apologize, but this year or right now, my focus is on growing, this side of my business. Maybe we can discuss this later. Can I call you in (month)?" Then schedule a specific time in the future to follow up.

You can also say, "In my affiliate program, I already have someone from your industry. Is it okay for me to hold on to your information and reach out to you when there's an opening?

Example 3: "I truly value and respect those in my network, so I don't share their information or connect them with people that I don't know. I would love to get to know you, so that we can work together.

"Vulnerability gives us freedom, power and connects us to a network of injured souls. It is through the art of being real that we can heal ourselves and others." ~ Shannon L. Alder

BEFORE THE EVENT

- ❑ Create your Purpose Brand
- ❑ Identify Your Target Market
- ❑ Develop a Unique Value Proposition and a 30 Second Award Winning Pitch
- ❑ Complete Your Brand Profile
- ❑ Complete Your 30-Day Pre-Networking Brand Checklist
- ❑ Leverage Your Existing Network
- ❑ Identify Additional Ways to Expand Your Network
- ❑ Complete Your Weekly Networking Strategic Plan

EQUIPMENT

Figure it out for yourself, my lad,
You've all that the greatest of men have had,
Two arms, two hands, two legs, two eyes
And a brain to use if you would be wise.
With this equipment they all began,
So start for the top and say, "I can."

Look them over, the wise and great
They take their food from a common plate,
And similar knives and forks they use,
With similar laces they tie their shoes.
The world considers them brave and smart,
But you've all they had when they made their start.

You can triumph and come to skill,
You can be great if you only will.
You're well equipped for what fight you choose,
You have legs and arms and a brain to use,
And the man who has risen great deeds to do
Began his life with no more than you.

You are the handicap you must face,
You are the one who must choose your place,
You must say where you want to go,
How much you will study the truth to know.
God has equipped you for life, but He
Lets you decide what you want to be.

Courage must come from the soul within,
The man must furnish the will to win.
So figure it out for yourself, my lad.
You were born with all that the great have had,
With your equipment they all began,
Get hold of yourself and say: "I can."

~ Edgar A. Guest

4 CREATING YOUR PURPOSE BRAND

And we know that in all things God works for the good of those who love him and have been called according to his purpose.
(Romans 8:28)

"When you are content to be simply yourself and don't compare or compete, everyone will respect you." ~ Lao Tzu

Everything you do is branding! You can't go anywhere today without seeing, hearing or being exposed to a brand. So what does branding have to do with networking? Everything! Having the right brand, helps you to stand out and grants you influence in a noisy, competitive marketplace. As a career seeker, it causes perspective clients and employers to see you the way you want to be seen. When it comes to your brand, you make the rules.

Your brand is basically your public image and promise of what you will deliver to a prospective client or employer. Good, bad are indifferent, your brand speaks to who you are and how you show up in your life and business. Brands are not

You teach people who you are, how to use and treat you.

only for businesses, but those seeking to build a lasting career. If you are unethical, greedy or rude, all of these identifiers can also attach themselves to or become your brand, so be mindful of the experiences you deliver when interacting with others. Your personal brand includes elements like your name, logo, a slogan, theme, design and the continual messages that you choose to deliver. A major component of your brand is the unique, consistent theme(s) that you create for yourself, business, and its products/ services. These themes help you to engage and capture the attention of your clients or employers. Your brand connects them to who you truly are and the value that you or your company add. Your personal brand sets you and your business apart in the marketplace.

pur·pose

the reason why something is done or used: the aim or intention of something: the aim or goal of a person: what a person is trying to do, become, etc.

Over the last few years, branding has become a trending subject, causing everyone to jump on the bandwagon, establishing their own brand. The issue with this is that many of them are smoke and mirrors. There are a lot of brands today that are simply hype, creativity and good marketing. Like a fake ID, most people pick a catchy name and title, put some creative marketing behind it and run with it. There have been many times that I have attended events and met someone that I was connected to on Facebook, Twitter or LinkedIn, only to find that their brand was great, but it didn't line up with who they really were. Because of all of the amazing resources that we have access to and technology, it's easy to create an amazing, but bogus brand.

As a result of my continuous interactions with people and businesses that didn't live up to or deliver on their brand promise, I began to wonder why this was happening. You must recognize that when you build a false brand that doesn't speak to who you truly are; you only end up hurting yourself. Developing a personal brand, that isn't authentic, keeps you from reaching and connecting with those you are called to serve. In an effort to help those lost souls with fake personal brands tap into their authenticity, I created *Purpose Branding*. A purpose brand speaks to who you are holistically and authentically. There's no guess work involved because its data driven, based on where you've been and where you're going. Your purpose brand includes your major life experiences (good & bad), accomplishments (results), your spiritual gifts, skills, strengths, talents, values, and personality. Add vision and a clear understanding of purpose to your brand and you'll find that market engagement is exponentially increased. For those that are growing a business, you can tie these elements into the personality and culture of the business.

A purpose brand is branding with purpose. It's a brand that has a voice and experience that moves people to act and has massive impact. Purpose brands are for those who want to create a movement around their brand. It's more than a creative, catchy name with great marketing; it's based on evidence and action. It's bigger than a job title or career path. It takes everything in your life into consideration (birth till this very moment). It doesn't just consider where you are but where you're going. It takes into consideration, your past, your dreams and your future – it's mission focused. Like many, I'm sure that you have asked yourself, what is my purpose? The bible tells us clearly that the reason we were created is for God's glory, so when I refer to purpose this is what I am speaking of. How do you give God the glory? You do it by surrendering to his will and being a vessel that he can use to move about the earth, reaching others through acts of love and service. Understand that your career or business is not your purpose, it's simply a vehicle that you can use to facilitate purpose. Often times when we talk about purpose, we confuse the how with the what. So now that you are clear on what your purpose is, let's get clear on the how, so that you can consistently deliver your brand time after time, making it easier to facilitate purpose. This will open doors and cause people to trust you, granting you favor and access like never before. Having a purpose brand will also help others know how to introduce, refer and connect you. I don't care who you are, someone is going to talk about you, but with a clear purpose brand, you give them what to say in the process. With a continual message being delivered in the marketplace you'll stand out and reach your target customer or employer faster.

STEP 01 — WHO AM I?

As you move through the following activities, do so without second guessing yourself. You must learn to live from your I know, that I know space. I truly believe that everyone knows exactly what they are called to do and be in life. The struggle is usually in seeing how to make it happen and get paid for it. Before you can establish your purpose brand, you must be very clear on who you are. It doesn't matter how small you think it is because every gift is significant when it comes to kingdom impact. Sometimes it's something really simple, but powerful. I am known for my ability to think strategically, my smile, energy, passion and my ability to speak into others' lives, unlocking spiritual identity, disrupting unproductive habits and stirring up their gifts. It's absolutely critical that you know your true, authentic self, key attributes and strengths. Your greatest opportunity for success and growth lie in identifying and operating in your gifts and strengths, so from this moment on, be aware of your weaknesses, but build on your strengths.

Career Seekers:

You must break the cycle of being tied to a title and connect to your true identity, so that you can pursue career options that feed you at your core and make you feel alive. Who you are and what you do can't be described by one specific title. Don't allow the world to limit you to something because it's what you have always done. Apply for jobs that you know you can do and that your life experiences have prepared you for, business and personal. Don't get discouraged when a position doesn't work. Keep pressing forward, fighting until you get the position you want. Understand that the testing of your faith produces perseverance. Work with a professional resume writer to strategically craft a resume that gets you the position you want.

When selecting an employer, you should select a company that aligns with your values and brand so that it's easy for you to be a brand ambassador for them.

ACTIVITY 1.1: Self-Assessment

Take out a notebook, a blank sheet of paper or use your computer to answer the following questions and complete the following activities.

- Start by listing your strengths, personality traits, talents, skills, hobbies, areas of expertise and the things that you are passionate about.

- What are you known for?

- What do you love to do?

- What things do you do that cause you to lose track of time?

- What is your WOW factor? What makes you stand out?

- Take 5 minutes to write as many words as you can to describe yourself. Don't think too much about your answers. When your 5 minutes are up, go through and circle any words or phrases that are mentioned two or more times. What words or phrases resonate with you and make you smile? You also want to merge any words or phrases that are similar or work together. Finally highlight your top five words in the list.

❏ Complete the following assessments to gain clarity on who you are. Review the assessments to see how the results align with your responses above. If there is alignment, you are on the right track with your brand. After completion, you will understand more about your personality and strengths. Don't complete all of the assessments in one day - schedule time for each one, so that you can focus. When completing the assessments, move through them quickly for authentic responses. Don't overthink your responses. After you have completed them, print and review your answers, highlighting the words and key phrases that resonate with you.

❏ Finally ask yourself, what do I want to be remembered for?

Assessments:

After you have completed each assessment listed below, go through and highlight/ circle words and phrases that resonate with you. You can use keys terms from these assessments to help you build your marketing message.

- ❏ DiSC Personality Assessment: www.discpersonalitytesting.com/free-disc-test
- ❏ Personality Hacker: www.personalityhacker.com
- ❏ Spiritual Gifts: http://www.spiritualgiftstest.com/test

ACTIVITY 1.2: Professional Assessment

Print your resume. Review your background and experience. Cross out the jobs, positions, roles and tasks that you dislike. Make notes as to why you disliked the tasks or positions that you marked through. If you don't have a resume, list your all current and past business, work and volunteer experiences in your notebook or on a blank sheet of paper and follow the same steps listed above.

Business Owners and Professionals:

If you're a business owner or considering starting a business, there might be opportunities for you to offer a solution to the marketplace using your skills, gifts, talents and experiences. If you're passionate and knowledgeable in a specific area, create a product or service.

❑ If you are running a business that you no longer enjoy, I encourage you to go through this process as well to seek ways to revamp your business. Review every product and service, note what's working and what isn't.

Career Seeker:

❑ If you're a career seeker, then your job would be to avoid these positions like the plague or find a position that allows you to do work you enjoy. For positions that you liked or enjoyed, highlight the specific tasks, assignments or accomplishments that brought you joy and make notes as to why. These are items that you want to look for in future positions

When searching online or in job banks, don't search by titles because many companies have started to get creative. Instead search by key words or terms associated with the career or work your desire to do. Search for jobs based on what you want, need or value. When I was searching for a position, I would search by words like engagement, flexibility, speaker, trainer, fun, peaceful, Christian, contract, work from home, membership, retention, coordinator, Jesus, ethical, life, love, etc. Search by things you want in and from a company, its environment or culture. You can also search for work based on your values.

Examples:

If you are a Speaker or Corporate Trainer, you can search using terms like, change, transformation, motivation, teacher, learning, etc.

If you value kindness, God, love, ministry, church, peace, Jesus, people, meditation, or stillness you can search for positions using these words.

ACTIVITY 1.3: Define Your Values

Identify and list the top five values that you live by. These values will help you gain clarity on what's truly important to you. They will help you establish the standards by which you will operate and keep you focused on what's important. Remember that life changes, so your values may change. If you need assistance, please visit www.movebeyondmotivation.com to view and print a full values list.

☐ Highlight all the words that resonate with you.

☐ Next, go back through the list and circle your top five values from those that you highlighted.

☐ Now, select your top 5 values and rank them in order of importance. Look up and write or type the definition of each value. Make note of why each value is important to you. Make these values visible in your home, business or office. You can even include them on your website and on social media platforms, in the about section.

STEP 02: HOW DO OTHERS SEE YOU?

Now for the moment of truth. Survey your customers, prospects, partners, family members and friends to see what they think of you and how they view you. This feedback is invaluable because it helps you to see what your existing brand is comprised of. Make sure that you only survey people that you know will provide truthful feedback, whether it's positive or negative. If one person says something, no need to focus on it, but if ten people say the same thing, you might want to pay attention to it. Also consider the things your friends and family consistently call you for help with? Write these things down. If you have received thank you notes, emails or feedback from customers, co-workers and other company leadership, review them to see if there are common themes present. This is your opportunity to see if others view you the way you view yourself. If the feedback you receive from the survey aligns with everything in step1, you're on the right track. If it doesn't, you have a lot of work to do.

ACTIVITY 2.1: External Assessment

Create a survey using Survey Monkey or Constant Contact because they will tabulate the results for you, saving you tons of time. Make sure that the survey is anonymous, so that participants will be truthful.

Keep the survey short and sweet. While you wait for these results, think of a time when someone thanked you or recognized you for something that made you stick your chest out and walk peacock proud. Identify an instance or multiple instances where you have made an impact or difference in someone's life that made you feel good or like you could conquer the world. The last time you received a thank you card, email message or letter, what did they thank you for?

Business Owners and Professionals:

❑ Send out an email with the survey link to a test group of clients, partners, affiliates, etc. (at least 10 to 15 contacts). If you're comfortable with it, send it to your entire client list. This survey is also a great opportunity to measure client satisfaction and value.

❑ You can also use a Facebook survey app or post questions on your social media channels asking your Facebook friends, Twitter followers and LinkedIn connections what they think of you. Please be careful with this method because in the instance that someone posts something negative its open for everyone to see. See the list of sample survey questions to consider below.

Career Seekers:

❑ If you are currently employed, request a copy of your quarterly or annual review that was completed by your supervisor, review this feedback.

❑ Survey your co-workers, family, friends and supervisors to see what they think about you?

❑ You can also send out an email to survey former employers and co-workers. You should also consider surveying those you work closely with, if you're currently employed.

Sample Survey Questions:

❑ List up to five words that you would use to describe me or my business.

❏ Why do you continue to do business with me? What do you like most about me and my business? What things do I do well? What areas need improvement? What do you like least? What improvements could be made to better serve you?

❏ What value do you receive from doing business with me?

❏ What services do I provide? What do you think I do?

❏ Ask questions about the things you think you do well.

Example: Do we provide good customer service? Rate our customer service on a scale of 1 to 10. There may be things that you think you're good at, but really aren't.

❏ Have I added value to your life? If so, how?

❏ How has being connected to me impacted your life?

ACTIVITY 2.2: Purpose Brand Summary

Review your responses from steps 1 and 2, highlight, circle and make notes as needed. Finally ask yourself...

☐ What recurring themes exist among all of your responses and the feedback you received.

☐ What comes naturally to you?

☐ What information was the most exciting to you?

- [ ] Am I currently using my gifts, talents and skills? Are you connecting your passions with your career, business, relationships or life? If not, how can you do this?

- [ ] What products and services can you add to your offering?

- [ ] What words or language can you use that will speak directly to your target customer, employer and partners? Remember to select words that grab the attention of those you serve and that will cause you to stand out in the marketplace.

- [ ] What did you learn about your passions, gifts, talents and skills?

Optional Activity:

When you establish your brand, will you be going by your name or a fun alias? Write down various options that align with your purpose, business name, and area of expertise, then circle or highlight your final choice.

Example: The Strategic Connector, the Mindset Shifter, Love Doctor, Vision Stirrer, Dream Coach, The Accountability Coach, etc. Whatever you choose, make sure you're not just being creative, but that it speaks to what you were called to do and the results you can achieve. Many times, we take on lives that our parents wanted us to have or we identify with the roles that people have assigned us to. Yes, I know that you are a mother, father, secretary, engineer, minister, friend, volunteer, intern, etc., but your greatest life role and title is being _____ (place your name in the blank), a disciple of Christ. All the roles and titles that you hold are just identifiers to help others know what jobs and tasks you are capable of performing.

Always remember that no matter how many hats or titles that you wear or have, your most important role and/ or title should be DISCIPLE.

IDENTIFY YOUR TARGET CUSTOMER OR EMPLOYER

There are over 7.3 billion people in the world. There is no way that you can afford to target everyone, if you expect to be successful in today's saturated marketplace. You must understand that everyone is not your customer, so don't allow these words to flow from your lips. You can no longer keep operating in business, like you're throwing pebbles into the ocean, trying to be everything to everybody. As a vessel you must understand that you are called and assigned to serve specific people and to meet specific needs. You must identify and define your target market, customer(s), partner(s) or employer, so that you are able to focus your marketing, sales and branding efforts to strategically speak to the group in which your products and services were created. As a part of your brand, you must really consider your brand voice and experience as a means of communicating and impacting the lives of your target customers. Because of technology, you are not only up against local competitors, but national ones as well. Clarity is critical when it comes to building and creating your purpose brand. Whether you're a business owner, professional or career seeker, you must know without a doubt who and what your ideal customers, strategic partners or employers look like. You must know who your target customer or employer is and what they look like to design a brand that holistically communicates with them to generate more targeted opportunities.

Before you dive into identifying your target customer, strategic partner(s) or employer, it's always easier for most people to identify what they don't want, so let's start there, so that you can make room for what you do want. Use your notebook to jot down your responses to the following activities. Don't second guess yourself, write from your core, listen to your heart and let your spirit guide you. The following activities will assist you in clearly identifying and orchestrating a visual of the people you were created to serve. They will also help you to develop your brand voice as a means of communicating with them.

ACTIVITY 3.1: Make Room for Your Best Clients

<u>Business Owners and Professionals</u>:

Identify your most painful customers and partners. If you're honest with yourself, we all have them. The ones that you need to fire because they drain the life out of you. What do they look like? When possible, you want to avoid these customers and partners like the plague and refrain from recruiting or working with them. These are the customers that drive you insane and cause your eyes to roll in the back of your head when you see their names pop up on the caller ID. During this activity, you will create a profile for the customer you aren't interested in acquiring or working with. If you have specific names, start with their name or business name, then underneath write what it is that you don't like and why. Make sure to keep this document at home, so that your staff or customers don't ever come across it. What you may find is that there isn't really a business, but a personal or personality issue. When you're in business for yourself, you must learn how to make decisions out of logic and not temporary emotions. At the end of this activity you must ask yourself, is it worth what they are paying me? If they are a higher maintenance client, you may also want to develop a higher priced product or service offering to make it worth your time.

<u>Career Seekers</u>:

Consider that company, internship or volunteer opportunity that you literally almost cried every day you rolled out of bed because you hated to go. Identify the job, where time dragged like you were watching paint dry. What do these employers look like? What was it that you couldn't stand about the company, the environment, your co-workers or its leadership? Studies show that most people leave companies because of the leadership. List all the characteristics, values, activities and behaviors you can think of.

ACTIVITY 3.2: Time for Release

Now it's time to be truthful with yourself. Before we identify your ideal customer, strategic partners or employer, you must remove the painful customers and employers from your life and business. These are customers, partners or employers that suck the life out of you. They drain you of time, energy and resources and you've clearly identified that it's not worth it. Before you make the decision to release them, only do so if you are 100% sure that it's them and not you. If it's a personal issue that can be resolved, please think through this and devise a plan to resolve it. The issue could be resolved by implementing better processes. Now if, you are 100% sure that you have no choice but to let them go, build your customer release or employee exit strategy, so that you can free up the time that is being poured into these relationships and/ or partnerships, so that you can access what's meant for you. Remember to be respectful and professional in the process.

Business Owners and Professionals:

Review your existing client list, write down the names of the customers and partners that you will need to release and follow your customer release strategy to transition them out of your business and life. Establish a date to have this process complete. Do it with dignity and honor, respecting the client throughout the process. Refer them to someone that you trust. Do not share your negative experiences in full detail. Decide on a professional statement to inform the client or partner that things have changed or that they are no longer a fit for you or your business.

Career Seekers:

If you're in a position that isn't providing you growth or fulfillment, whether that's as an employee, volunteer or intern, you must decide on your transition date. Go ahead and write your letter of resignation. Have it ready to go. As you plan for transition, you must do it with excellence. List all of the things you can do to make sure that the person replacing you can pick up where you left off. Complete these tasks as you prepare for transition. Organize your folders to make accessing things easier. Do not delete everything on your computer. If you are a disgruntle employee, you must work through releasing this as you will carry it into your next position if you don't.

Now that you've cleared your life and business of clutter and gotten the hard stuff out of the way, let's get down to business. Before getting started, get clear on what it is that you do want in your life, business and career. What does your ideal customer, strategic partner or employer look like?

ACTIVITY 3.3: Customer Intake & Assessment Forms

Do what you can to avoid working with the wrong customers or partners. Be a little more strategic. Sure, there may be a time or two that one slips through the cracks, but for the most part implementing a screening processes will limit this occurrence.

Business Owners and Professionals:

Develop and implement customer intake, booking and assessment forms to qualify and weed out customers that are not a good fit for you and your business. These forms are used to assess customer needs, values, service standards and goals, while establishing compatibility and weeding out what you don't want in your business. If you need assistance with developing forms for your business, please contact us at admin@movebeyondmotivation.com.

Career Seekers:

As you go on interviews, remember that the interview is just as much for you as it is for them. You have to do your homework before the interview to prepare questions that will help you identify whether or not the company is the right fit for you. In addition to
basic salary, job responsibility and time questions, ask questions like the following.

- What do you like most about working here?

- Based on your experiences how would you describe the culture here? What's your leadership style?

- What's your DiSC personality type or leadership style?

- Do you provide ongoing growth and development training? Does the company have tuition reimbursement?

Ask questions about the things that truly matter to you. Also, don't forget to get the names of those interviewing you, so that you can send them a thank you note or connect with them on LinkedIn. Even if you don't get the job, you can stay connected with them for future opportunities. Remember you should always be seeking opportunities to connect.

❑   You also want to do your due diligence in interviewing the person that you will be reporting to – assess their personality, attitude, and leadership style to ensure that you all are a great fit for each other.

ACTIVITY 3.4: Your Target Customer Profile

<u>Business Owners and Professionals</u>:

List your top 10 to 20 customers that you enjoy working with. You must be able to recognize the customers that you want more of. Think about what they look like? Why do you love working or interacting with them?

❑ Who currently uses your products and services? What are their needs and desires?

❑ What do they value?

❑ What connects you to them?

❑ How are you like your ideal customer?

❑ Why did you create each product or service?

❑ What problem did you aim to solve?

❑ Who did you have in mind when you created it?
❑ What do the people that have this problem look like?

Strategic Partner Profile:

❑ Identify those in your network that have products and services that compliment yours.

- ❏ Who has an ideal customer that resembles yours? Who can add value to your customers?

- ❏ Do their values, mission, vision, values and work ethic compliment or align with yours.

This is also a great opportunity to profile inbound and outbound referral partners? Inbound referral partners are those that refer clients to you, while outbound referral partners are those that you trust to refer business to when you have more clients than you can handle or as the result of a strategic referral partnership.

Career Seekers:

If you are seeking employment, when someone asks you what you're looking for, don't say "Anything, I just need a job." Make them aware of what you're passionate about and what your background is in relation to the type of position you're seeking. Don't just give someone a title because employers have gotten creative with titles, so you might miss a great opportunity.

Relentlessly pursue what you want in your life, business and relationships.

Also keep in mind that as you are searching, it's okay to accept a "meantime" position, but don't get comfortable or give up on your search. Never allow yourself to get stuck in a meantime situation, as meantime indicates that you're just passing through. Also, if you have the work or life experience, don't let not having the education stop you. Where there's a will, there's a way.

Career seekers, ask yourself the following questions.

- ❏ Consider past companies, internships and volunteer opportunities you like, enjoy or love? What did you like or love about them? What was the environment like? What kind of co-workers did you have? This will give you an idea of what to look for in your next role.

❑ What industry do you want to work in or with? What industries are you knowledgeable of or have you enjoyed working in?

❑ What type of company or industry best aligns with your vision? Always make career moves based on your future – your vision, goals and where you desire to be?

❑ Do you want to work for a big or small firm?

❑ What job tasks do you want to perform?

❑ What is your area of expertise? What skills, talent or experience are these employers seeking? Where will your skills be best utilized?

❑ What type of company culture do you want to be a part of?

❑ If it's a specialized industry, what do they value? What results are they seeking?

❑ What city or state do you want to work in? How far are you willing to commute?

❑ Do you want flexibility? What hours do you want to work? Always select a company that aligns with the type of life you want to live and your values.

ACTIVITY 3.5: Dig Deeper: Target Customer Profile

Need a little more assistance establishing your target customer or employer profile, take a moment to work through the following questions.

Demographic Characteristics:

- Gender: Men, Women or Both?
- Age or Age Range?
- Relationship Status: Married? Single?
- Children: Gender and Age?
- Family Size:
- Education Level: GED, High School, Technical School, College, Masters, or PhD?
- Career or Profession: Entry-Level, Supervisor, Manager, Director, Executive, CEO?
- Income or Range:
- Are they business owners? What stage of business are they in?
- What books or magazines do they read?

Geographic Characteristics

- If they are business owners, where are their businesses located?
- If they are professionals or individuals, where do they live and work?
- Where do they live?

Psychographic Characteristics

- Why do they buy specific products?
- What are their spending habits?

Behavioral Characteristics:

When, where, why and how do they buy?

Other Questions:

<u>Business Owners and Professionals</u>:

- ❑ What are their biggest issues or challenges?
- ❑ What is the core solution that you provide for this ideal client?
- ❑ Why would they choose to buy your products and services, instead of your competitors?
- ❑ What mind-blowing benefits or results will they receive from purchasing and utilizing your product or service? It's important that you focus on the benefits and results.

Career Seekers:

What value do I provide to my employer and co-workers? What unique skills, talents or experience do I have? Be strategic, review your experiences to see how your life and business back ground aligns. Don't just look at activities. You can also look at what your co-workers, managers and customers consistently say about what they appreciate and value about you.

ACTIVITY 3.6: Identifying a Niche Market (Optional)

Do you want to go deeper and get laser focused?

Identify Your Niche.

Example: If you are a manufacturer of metal parts. Your target market is companies that use metal parts to manufacture products. Your niche market may be manufacturing companies with military contracts to build bombs.

Ask yourself these additional questions...

- ❑ Are there any unmet needs that are not being met by your competitors, but that you have the capacity to meet?

❑ Is there any additional value that you could add?

❑ Are there any products or services mentioned in the survey that should be discontinued because of substantial negative feedback? Are there any products and services that should be added?

ACTIVITY 3.7: Target Profile Summary

Go back through the last five activities and highlight everything that stands out to you, in relation to your target customer, partner or employer. What are your must haves? Now, complete your target profile - write a full description. Get as detailed as possible using the characteristics you highlighted and the info you listed by answering the prior questions.

STEP 04: ESTABLISH YOUR UNIQUE VALUE PROPOSITION

You must deliver a clear and consistent message to engage your target audience and stand out. People are constantly inundated with marketing messages throughout the day, so you must use strategic words to grab their attention.

Now that you have identified your target customer or employer, you must create an eye-popping value proposition or marketing message. Avoid being just person in a category by clearly understanding what's at the core of your target customers or employers wants and needs.

This allows you to effectively communicate with them and grab their attention immediately. This is why it's in your best interest to create a Unique Value (Selling) Proposition (UVP) and an *Award-Winning Pitch* (AWP) that communicates the value that you provide. Competing, selling and delivering products and services in a heavily saturated market is extremely difficult for those companies that don't have a unique value proposition. Your UVP will be your main way of communicating in every day networking situations, while your AWP will be reserved for conventional networking events or opportunities where people want more details. In most networking situations you only have a moment to grab the attention of a prospective client or employer. You're UVP and AWP both communicate the unique results or benefits that you offer and details why your customer or employer would choose you over the competition. Your UVP is the foundation of effective and impactful marketing activities. It communicates and delivers a clear, evidence-based statement that quantifies the value that you add to your customers via your skills, gifts, products, services and any experiences that they have with you or your brand. This is why you must learn to be consistent and extremely specific when you're communicating the benefits of your company, products, services and your brand. It's no longer enough to say, "We offer great customer service, cheap prices or fast delivery because everyone else is saying these same, basic things. Use phrases and taglines that others aren't using and that your customers and employers understand. Use your brand voice to speak their language.

Your clients and employers want results and that's why they hire you. With that being said, you must be able to always communicate the results you deliver and what sets you apart from everyone else as it relates to specifically what the client or employer has need of. Many times, we over sell ourselves or our products because we want to run down the list of all the great products and services we have or all of our skills versus listening, accessing the need and strategically speaking to the client or employers immediate need? For every benefit you have, it must have a WOW factor? Your goal is to pique their interest, so that they want to know more. The same applies to employees, what sets you apart? Think outside the box. Use engaging words that they understand, don't regularly hear as to grab their attention. Be bold in communicating what makes you, your product or service unique. Spice up their language. What have you heard them say in communicating their frustrations or pain points.

As you complete the following activities, list everything that comes to mind, providing as much detail as possible. If you need assistance generating your message, please contact us at admin@movebeyondmotivation.com.

ACTIVITY 4.1: Scripting Your Unique Value Proposition

<u>Business Owners and Professionals</u>:

☐ List every product and service offering that you have. Next to it or underneath it, write down the value that the customer gets from using it.

☐ What specific solutions do you offer to solve your client's problems?

☐ Why should your target customers purchase your products and services instead of your competitors?

☐ How does the product or service change, improve or enhance their life?

☐ How does it make them feel? How does it change their life or circumstances?

<u>Career Seekers</u>:

List everything that you believe makes you unique in the workplace. Next to it or underneath it, write down the value that your employer or customers receive from it.

❑ What specific solutions do you offer to solve your employer's problems?

❑ How do you add value to the company? List everything that comes to mind.

❑ How do you work with others? How do you make them feel?

Again, provide as much detail as possible. Jot down ideas until you have a moment of complete surety and a smile over takes your face because it's perfect and resonates with every inch of your being. Refine your value proposition until you can articulate it in a single, credible sentence or slogan. You want to have a go to slogan that speaks to your overall value proposition, but you can also have multiple product and service-based slogans for those instances that you are focused on growing a specific product, service or area of your business.

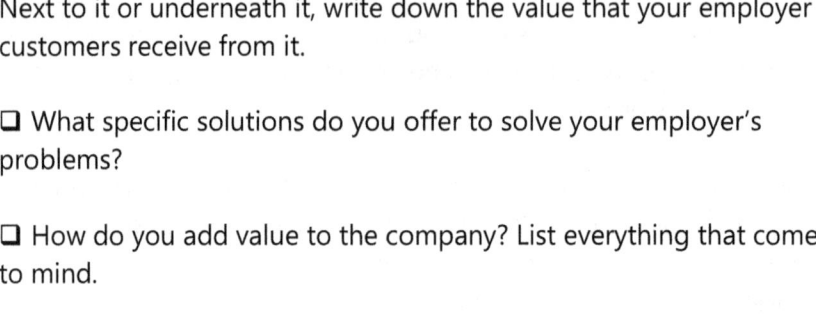

Tip: Google your competitors, those that resemble your business. See what they are saying and offering. It's not necessarily about being different from them, but being yourself and tying who you are into your offerings. Always keep in mind, when compared to them, what will separate you?

STEP 05 — CRAFT YOUR AWARD WINNING PITCH

The standard for networking pitches is about 30, no more than 60 seconds long. It should be short and engaging, describing what you do, who you do if for, what problems you solve and the results you provide. To enhance your pitch, throw a special, complimentary offer in at the end. Be very careful of using the word free because everything has a cost, even if it's time. Your *Award-Winning Pitch* should be tailored to your audience, so consider this each time that you attend a networking event. Don't forget to say your name and company name at the beginning and the end of your pitch. The following are things you may want to include in your pitch. Remember these are only guidelines. This is your pitch, so create what makes you feel good.

ACTIVITY 5.1: Compile Your Pitch

Write a draft and edit it until it flows and makes you smile.

I **ACTION VERB**

- ❑ **WHO** is your target customer, partner or employer?

- ❑ **WHAT** problems do they face? Name two to three issues.

- **HOW** do you solve their problems and what unique solutions do you provide to meet their needs?

- **RESULTS:** What key benefits or solutions have you provided for your existing clients? This should be something that blows their mind and makes others want to do business with you.

- **OPPORTUNITY:** Offer something complimentary to drive them to take action.

Pitch Examples:

Divorce Attorney: I help wealthy families that have a lot to lose, navigate the difficult, life altering process of divorce with dignity and fairness. I help couples respectfully divorce, so that they can successfully co-parent, while peacefully and fairly negotiating their assets. We have over 200 clients with a 95% satisfaction rate. Contact me today for a free review of your assets.

Website Designer: I help small business owners and entrepreneurs create affordable websites that speak to their brand, have powerful calls-to-action that drive consumers to make massive purchases. All of our clients have exceeded their online sales goals this year by 35%. See me after the event for a $100 off website design services.

After you have written your pitch, you are ready to start using it. You can even craft a few different versions to try out before you settle on the one that works. Now, share it with the world. When you deliver your pitch, it must come out sounding natural and confident. Practice out loud, repeatedly in front of a mirror, paying close attention to your words, facial expressions and body language. Many times words sound good on paper, but not as profound when said out loud. Saying your pitch aloud helps you find a more conversational way to deliver your message. As you practice your pitch, make sure that you aren't rushing through it, look for areas of emphasis or maximum impact. Make sure that you speak at a pace that enables prospective customers to absorb what you're saying.

Career Seekers:

Be clear about the position you are seeking, beyond the title. What things or activities are important to you? Think about the position you have now. What do you like about it? Write down these keys words. Look at the things you highlighted and noted in your resume, use keywords that you have identified. You should also search by your skills, gifts and talents to see what pops up.

If no one will give you a job, create one!

STEP 06: COMPLETE YOUR BRAND PROFILE SUMMARY

Use all of the information you compiled from each step to build your brand. BE COMPLETELY HONEST WITH YOURSELF!

ACTIVITY 6.1: SUM IT UP

❏ At the core of your Purpose Brand, will be answers to the following questions.

❏ What's your area of expertise, even if you aren't currently or ever been paid for it?

❏ What do you want to be known for?

❏ Who are you, holistically and authentically?

- ❑ What are you passionate about?
- ❑ What specific problems do you feel that you created to solve?
- ❑ What have you been through and overcome, so you want to help others do the same?
- ❑ Who were you created to serve and why?
- ❑ What makes you unique?
- ❑ What things frustrate you or make you mad? What solutions can you provide?

YOUR PRE-NETWORKING PURPOSE BRAND CHECKLIST

BUILD & ENGAGE YOUR NETWORK THROUGH YOUR BRAND

Now that you have identified your purpose brand, it's extremely important that everything you are and deliver to the world, speaks to your brand. Create a document that houses your brand profile and guidelines. Truly consider your audience and create marketing materials that speak to them and their needs. Once these items are compiled, save it in a pdf document and share it with your staff and partners to help ensure consistency in your brand delivery to the marketplace. Check out a few samples on my website. Great resources for marketing material creation -www.fiverr.com and www.canva.com.

❑ **The Brand:** Your Name or business name

❑ **Main Contact/ Brand Name:** Your name and alias

❑ **Business Location** (Address, city and state):

❑ **Phone Number:**

❏ **Voicemail:** Record a fun, engaging voicemail message that includes your value proposition and brand messaging. Call me at 972.672.8873 to hear an example.

❏ **Website:** Update your existing website to speak to your new/ updated brand. If you don't have one, create and launch one. Hire a professional if needed, but there are so many great existing templates that you can use. Check out www.wix.com. Your website should at a minimum have the following pages: home, bio or about me, services/ products, and contact information. Feel free to add any additional pages or features at any time. Be creative! Add videos to your website. If you haven't done so already, register your domain name.

❏ **Sales & Marketing Plan/ Calendar:** Outline and develop a sales and marketing strategy. Complete your social media marketing calendar. Content is key to engaging your online contacts. Start by placing all of the events and meetings that you have for the month on the calendar. How can you use them and what can you post in relation to them to enhance your brand and engage your network? Post a picture of the event and share an experience. Every post should invite your audience into your life and business, making them feel as if they are right there with you. Don't forget to establish a budget.

❏ **Clothing:** What's your style? How will you dress? What is required by the environments you are in?

Social Media Platform Links: For branding purposes, you want all of your brand/ about info and page names to be consistent. Use www.namechk.com to check the availability of your name or business name on various social media platforms. For example, I am kishalallen on all channels except Facebook because my name wasn't available, so I am kishalallen1. Connect with me.

❑ **Facebook:** Create an account at www.facebook.com and complete your full profile. Upload a professional headshot, an engaging timeline cover, customize your tabs, bio, etc.

❑ **LinkedIn:** Create an account at www.linkedin.com. Go through each section until your full profile is complete. Add a professional profile photo. Don't forget to add YouTube videos. www.linkedin.com.

❑ **Instagram:** Create and brand an account at www.instagram.com.

❑ **Pinterest:** Create and brand an account at www.pinterest.com.

❑ **Twitter:** Create an account at www.twitter.com, complete your profile, add a professional headshot, and update your background and layout to be reflective of your brand and brand color scheme.

❑ **YouTube:** Create a channel at www.youtube.com, then add promo videos for your products, services and company. Create 3 to 5 videos on various subjects in your industry. Videos are critical to enhancing your visibility and becoming a subject matter expert. Use keywords to your video titles and descriptions. Don't forget to add your website to the description. Use www.fiverr.com to create a promo video or to get your videos distributed for $5. Make videos with other experts. Schedule one day a week minimum to record a video.

❑ **Hootsuite or Buffer**: Create an account at www.hootsuite.com or www.buffer.com. It's up to you to decide which platform is best for you; both are social media account management tools that allow you to manage your social media accounts in one place. You can also use them to preschedule posts.

❑ **Additional Online Exposure:** Create an account and follow the step by step guide to update your full brand profile on www.brandyourself.com and www.about.me, and www.klout.com.

❑ **Logo(s):** Design and select a logo to represent your brand. Contact a graphic designer for assistance designing a logo that speaks to your brand. If it's simply your name, what does this look like? Use www.fiverr.com for low cost services. I would suggest having a horizontal and a vertical version. Add your new logo, slogan and color scheme to your business card, letters, labels, note cards, and envelops.

❏ **Pictures:** Take, high quality, professional photos/ headshots to be used on your website and social media profiles.

❏ **Banners:** Website and Social Media

❏ **Brand Colors (RGB, HSL and Color Code):** Go to http://www.usabilitypost.com/2008/09/29/a-guide-to-choosing-colors-for-your-brand for more info on selecting your brand colors. After you have decided which colors to use, go to www.html-color-codes.info or www.htmlcolorcodes.com/color-picker/ to get color numbers for brand consistency.

❏ **Font(s) Used – Name(s) and Size:**

❏ **Mission, Vision and Values:**

❏ **Areas of Expertise/ Experience:**

❏ **Your Target Customer Attributes:**

❏ **Unique Value Proposition/ WOW Factor:**

❏ **Your Brand Promise & Experience:** What experience and results do you deliver? You will also want to establish your client service guidelines. This can be a brief or detailed as you like. You can also use this data to create your client intake form and assessment.

❏ **Accomplishments, Certifications & Awards:** Use only those that support your brand.

❑ **Bio (Business & Individual:** Write a new bio that is reflective of your brand. This info will be used in your website About area and on your social media platforms.

❑ **Client Testimonials** (3 to 5): Contact clients that are absolutely pleased with your work and request a 3 to 5 sentence testimonial that speaks to their experience with you, the results and your expertise. Get 3 to 5 testimonials to start. If you have a LinkedIn account, you can request them here because you can copy and paste them or screenshot them.

❑ **Your Voice/ Tone:** Outline conversation starters and questions that speak to your brand. These questions should pique the interest of your customers, employers and those you network with. They should drive them to want to know more about who you are, your products/ services and what you do. How do you greet others? Do you have a saying or phrase that people associate you with?

❑ **Public Relations:** Create and send out an email and upload your press release to various media sites. Use www.prweb.com and www.everything-pr.com. When promoting your new brand, look at what's trending and find a way to tie your bran into hot topics.

❑ **Marketing Materials:** Design, print and order items like – signage, retractable banners, postcards, brochures, a press kit, rack cards, etc. to have them readily available for networking.

❑ **Blog:** Design your blog to represent your brand. Write valuable content that establishes you as an expert in your field. Link your blog to your website. www.wordpress.com. If you struggle with writing, start a video blog.

❑ **Google Alerts:** Set up Google Alerts for your name, topics of interest, your business name or keywords in your industry. This is a great way find content and stay connected to the things going on in your industry. http://www.google.com/alerts.

☐ **Letters:** Mail or email a letter introducing your new brand to your clients, partners, colleagues, prospects, etc. Have greater impact, by including a promotional item that is representative of your brand. Include all of your social media information in this piece to invite your contacts to connect with you online. This is also a great opportunity to promote a sale, a new product or service offering. Select an attention grabbing subject line. Use something that's currently trending to influence your subject line.

Expressing Your Brand in Your Event Experience

If you host events, design your event experience from arrival to exit.

☐ How will you generate leads?

☐ Outline the agenda/ run of show – add intended outcomes.

☐ Consider venue set-up – how are products, services and brand messages displayed throughout the event. Venue?

☐ Do you have special branded parking spaces or offer valet?

☐ Are your customers greeted at the door?

☐ Is your staff working the room? If you don't have staff, do you hire staff or get volunteers?

☐ What does the event forum look like?

☐ Will you recognize key community leaders or officials?

☐ Will you have VIP seating?

☐ Is everyone greeted when they leave and handed info or a gift?

Expressing Your Brand in Your Office Experience

❑ Arrange your office to be reflective of your brand - add your brand color scheme and accents.

❑ Properly display brand marketing messages, products and services throughout your office.

❑ Script your office experience - what does it look and feel like?

❑ Are guests greeted when they arrive, handed a beverage and something to read. Where would you like them seated?
❑ Is there light, mediation, symphony, pop, hip-hop, country or gospel music playing?

❑ Do guests leave with something in hand? Iron out the full details of the experience.

TIP: To ensure success, always schedule time for planning - add a daily reminder to your calendar to allocate time for branding and networking activities. You can use your Outlook, cell phone or printed calendar...whichever you utilize for success. If you don't currently manage a calendar, you can create one in excel. You can also, check out www.harvest.com to use their online time management tool. If you're stuck, visit my website www.movebeyondmotivation.com to schedule a strategy session.

5 NETWORKING IS EVERYWHERE

I get excited about what the Holy Spirit is doing now through all the people he is refining and raising up all over this planet. I love connections, relationship and networking, but it must be led by the Spirit. ~ Daniel Smith

EVERYTHING YOU HAVE NEED OF IS IN YOUR NETWORK!

To avoid missing out on what God has preordained, we must stop setting limits when it comes to networking. Networking is happening everywhere you go, whether you realize it or not. It's even happening right now as you go through this book, you and I are connecting with every word, further solidifying our relationship. The opportunities that you have each day to network are so astronomical that I won't be able to cover them all in this book. Literally, every time you read a post, comment, pass, stand next to or are in the same room with at least one additional person there's an opportunity for networking. So, from this day forward you have to promise me that you will no longer reserve networking to "networking events." If you are truly serious about living on purpose and reaching your destiny, every time you encounter another person, you will smile and greet them. Remember this when you are out to dinner or at an event. Every day and in everything you do, you should be seeking opportunities to network and connect.

We can't discuss networking without discussing the wealth of opportunities that technology offers, granting you worldwide access. We have more access to people and information than ever before, so the possibilities are endless and even more exciting is the fact that there are more than enough opportunities for everyone.

Six Degrees of Separation Theory

In 1929, write Frigyes Karinthy proposed the *Six Degrees of Separation theory*, which implies that everyone on earth is never more than approximately five people (degrees) away from meeting or connecting with any other person on the earth. Thanks to technology this theory is now truer than ever, allowing you to connect with anyone across the globe.

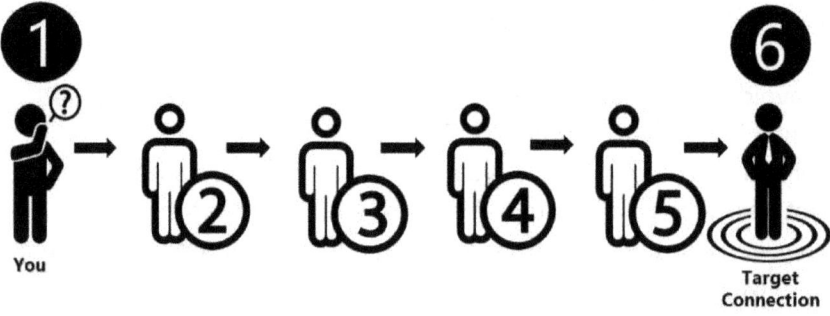

LEVERAGE YOUR EXISTING NETWORK

So where do you start?

Right where you are, leveraging your existing network.

Over my career, I have noticed that the most successful people are good at connecting, pursing opportunities and collaborating with others. While you're out chasing more connections to grow your network, they are leveraging their existing relationships, growing their networks naturally from the inside out. Your network is a goldmine. Everything you need to achieve success is a phone call, email, video chat or post away. If it's not accessible via an immediate connection, I promise you that they know someone who has it. Before you run out pursuing new opportunities, navigate your existing network first. Remember you were created for them and they were created for you. I truly believe that the people you are connected to truly want to see you win, they are just waiting for you to tell them what you have need of. You already have everything you need at your fingertips to be successful, so start with what you already have, working your way from the inside out. Start with the group(s) you're most connected to.

<u>Business Owners and Professionals:</u>

❏ Start by identifying those within your network that match up with your target customer and strategic partner profiles.

❏ If you have established goals, review them and list everything you have need of to achieve success. Next go through your network to identify people who have access to what you need or that can connect you to someone who does. Think through what this conversation should sound like (script it). Finally, contact them and MAKE THE ASK.

Example:

As a business owner or sales professional, if you have a $100,000 sales goal, what's the plan and the real opportunities to make this a reality? You could reach this goal through developing an affiliate program or hosting training events and selling products/ services at the end, having a booth at an event, selling on social media, etc. The list of ways to accomplish this one task are endless. If you decide to go the route of strategic or affiliate partners, you will need to find those in your network who fit the profile and have businesses whose product or service mix compliments yours. Connect with those whose target customer looks like yours and who can add value to your customers.

❑ Review your network to find prospective customers in which to network. Before starting this process, don't forget to merge all of your contacts from your email inbox and add all business cards to your social media platforms or CRM database. Scroll through cell phone lists, search databases and social media channels. In instances where exporting information is available, export data into spreadsheets for easier filtering and sorting. Remember to consider your capacity when taking on this task. Start with those that are closest to you, working your way through your network. How many contacts can you manage at one time? In an effort to find your flow and figure out what works, start by identifying your top 10 prospects. Ideally for effective networking you want to develop an engagement plan that includes an email marketing campaign. This will help you stay connected with and indirectly follow-up with multiple contacts at one time. Develop a separate plan for key prospects that includes direct contact initiatives.

❑ Outline your contact, sales and follow-up processes. If you don't have a CRM system in place, get one. Check out the CRM resources listed on page 136. Utilize your database to track contact interaction notes; use your calendar, if your database doesn't have a reminder feature to add follow-up notifications. This is important for managing relationship, existing and prospective.

❑ Create simple, professional, strategic and engaging offers that speak to your target customer. Create specific collateral with marketing messages directed at strategic and affiliate partners. Make sure that your unique value proposition, product and service offerings are clear. You also want to make sure that your marketing kit is complete and ready to go with all the necessary scripts, pricing, onboarding process, contracts and forms.

❑ Finally, take action, dive in, engage, serve, share and stay connected, engage prospective and existing customers and partners, **make the ask and follow up.** Be consistent and persistent.

Career Seekers:

❑ Start with those in your network, who either work in the field or work for the specific companies that you are targeting. Also make a list of all of the human resource representatives in your network. Review your target career and employer profiles, if needed. Remember that the key to networking is to be bold and like Nike says, JUST DO IT! Network and connect with an open heart and mind. You were created to do this! It all starts with a smile and hello.

❑ When you're seeking a job opportunity, send out an email to everyone you know, making them aware of your search. Tell them what you do, specifically what you're looking for and who you're looking to connect with. Attach your resume and cover letter to the email. Request that they share it with others within their network. Again be as specific as possible. Make sure that your resume and cover letter are professional, so they don't mind sharing it.

 As you review the opportunities on the next few pages, don't get overwhelmed. Pace yourself. Use this list as a resource to be strategic in reaching your goals. If you need to start off small and take it easy, that's okay. Again remember, JUST DO IT! Your goal should simply be to do one thing

every day to get you closer to accomplishing your goals and reaching destiny.

(1) College Networks (Alumni Groups, Fraternities and Sororities):

Every college has an alumni network. They host tons of events throughout the year to keep their alumni engaged. Identify events and groups, join, get involved and connect. Alumni networks are great for generating sales and career leads. Many alumni networks have job boards as well. A great networking strategy is to put your alumni, fraternity, sorority or college logos in your email signature and list it on your social media profiles. Search for these networks on social media, like their pages and join their groups. Interact, like, post and engage others as much as possible. When you see others wearing school paraphernalia, engage them.

(2) Co-workers, Supervisors, and Other Company Leadership (Former and Current): For those of you that say, "I don't go to work to make friends," stop it because while you may not go to make friends, it's in your best interest to be friendly. Often times, we don't recognize the value of connecting and establishing trust in the workplace. Your co-workers are a great network to have as a resource to accomplish tasks at work or to advance within the company. If you are an entrepreneur, they are also prospective customers. Have you ever needed something from the marketing department and their project list is 6 weeks long, but you needed your stuff yesterday? Being connected to others moves them to do special things for you, to go out of their way, to make sure you get what you need because they value, trust and respect you. This also comes in handy, when you apply for a different position within a company, even if they don't know your name, they know you as the guy or the lady that's always happy or the one that talks to everybody. Imagine going in to the interview and hearing, "Oh it's you, I didn't know your name," when they see you, opening the door to a new department or position. Also keep in mind that when you're connected, you communicate better, so you're plugged into everything that's going on because you're the one everyone wants to talk to. And don't forget that everyone you work with has a network as well, so connecting with them, connects you to everyone they know. It baffles me how many companies and sales people don't utilize their staff to generate sales leads.

Business Owners & Professionals:

❑ If you're an ex-employee, pursuing entrepreneurship or someone that runs a business while working a 9 to 5, make your co-workers aware of this when the conversation arises, you'll be surprised how many support you. **Make sure that your services don't compete with that of your employer or aren't a conflict of interest**. Reward them for referrals that turn into business.

❑ If you're in sales, ask employees to provide you with referrals. Remember to be specific when telling them who you want to be connected to. Speak with company leadership about implementing an employee referral rewards program.

Career Seekers:

❑ After you have submitted your letter of resignation, send an email out to your professional network, making them aware of your new career search. Tell them what you do, specifically what you're looking for and who you're looking to connect with. Attach your resume and cover letter to the email. The easier you make it, the more apt they are to share. In that email, ask them to put their feelers out in their networks. If you are still employed and looking, you can still do this, just make sure that your current supervisor, customers or those you work with aren't in your professional contact list.

❑ Connect with other career seekers to share opportunities that you find during your search. Work together and share opportunities that you come across during your search that match their target profile, ask that they do the same for you.

❑ Identify a mentor, someone that is in a position or role that you are interested in learning more about; connect with them and ask that they mentor you.

 **TIP:** If you like your existing company and the issue is simply that you need to make more money, don't pursue another career opportunity without first exploring the opportunities for advancement and asking for what you want/ need. Schedule a meeting with your supervisor and during this meeting, make him or her aware of your desire for growth. Ask if there are any opportunities for advancement and ask for his or her help in devising an advancement plan.

(3) Existing Customers: Implement a touch plan that keeps you connected to them. Pay attention for upsell opportunities.

(4) Former Customers: There are former customers that love you and your products/ services, but for one reason or another no longer do business with you. They may have left for financial reasons, life events or their needs changed. If you had a good relationship with a former customer and you've added a new product or service, reach out to them if you believe it's of value to them. Reconnect with former customers and implement a winback campaign. If they never opted out of your email/ e-newsletter list, keep them on to notify them of new product and service launches.

(5) Friends and Family Members: Keep in mind that your *familial network* is critical and most times overlooked. This is the first and most valuable network that God has provided you with. One of the hardest things about growing up with someone is that oftentimes they have the propensity to overlook and devalue you, as a result of familiarity. You have to recognize and honor the gifts, talents and skills that exist within your family and you'll see an increase in momentum as each of you are propelled into destiny. We must work to nurture and grow our *familial networks*, much like we do our professional network, becoming brand ambassadors and extended sales force for each other. To do this, start by making sure that all of your family members and friends know and clearly understand what you do and the value that you provide to the world. You must also know what they do. Your family knows you better than anyone on this earth and if no one will do business with or refer you, surely they will. If your own family refuses to do business with you or send business your way, then there's a problem and you may want to ask why so that you can fix it. Find out what companies your family and friends work for and if they fit your target customer profile, ask them to facilitate a connection or share your information with the appropriate contact. And don't forget to do the same for them.

Tip: Schedule a weekly conference call with your family via www.freeconferencecall.com. My family and I dial in every Monday at 8:30 PM to pray, study scripture, encourage each other, share good news and help each other find resources. Often times we focus on generational curses, when we should spend just as much time focused on nurturing generational gifts. It's time that your family reconnected and had these types of conversations. What you decide to do on your family call is up to you, just stay connected.

(6) HR Directors and Operations Managers- If the company is hiring or firing, someone in this capacity would know, so they can make you aware of and connect you to opportunities.

Business Owners & Professionals:

Keep in mind that struggling businesses offer great opportunities for business and sales consultants. If they are struggling, they need you to get their businesses back on track.

Career Seekers:

It goes without saying...connect with HR professionals, connect to job opportunities. HR professionals know others in the industry as well, so connect with them, connect with their network.

(7) Strategic Partners: Identify value enhancing partners and develop a referral exchange network of your own, like a BNI group that you meet with periodically to exchange contacts, resources and ideas. Start small and grow organically. Select partners that can provide increased or additional value to your customers. You may also want to partner with those who do what you do. so that when you are in your season of overflow and you have more business than you can handle, you will have trusted partners in which to refer clients. Even though many of us are in the same business, we all bring different skills, gifts, backgrounds and talents to the table. When partnering with complimentary companies, respect them and do not steal their clients. Consider establishing relationships with bankers, accountants, real estate agents, commercial brokers, and sales representatives. They are a great source for leads.

(8) Vendors: Those Who Serve You: This includes your lawn company, stylist, hair dresser/ barber, your favorite restaurants/ caterers, your car repair/ salesman, etc. These people are connected to tons of people, so they are a great group to establish a referral network with, especially if their target market aligns with yours; connect them to those in your network. Exchange a stack of business cards with them to place in your business and ask that they do the same.

NETWORKING ONLINE

This is such a huge topic to cover, so I am going to only cover the most common platforms and a few basic ways to utilize them to engage and expand your network. With social media, it's not enough to have thousands of likes, connections, followers or friends, you must engage them consistently. Remember to use your time wisely on these platforms because it's easy to get drawn in and find yourself still there five hours later. Your social media channels are a treasure chest filled with opportunities and a sales goldmine. Keep your eyes open because there is something to post about everywhere you go and in

When posting, be consistent and work to post content that supports and reinforces your brand.

everything you do. Your connections basically give you everything you need to wheel them in. These platforms allow you access into a prospect or existing customer's personal life. There are people all over your timeline and newsfeeds that are having babies, getting married, celebrating a birthday, going on vacation, and sharing other life events. These are opportunities to engage and connect and generate leads every day. Social media connections don't have to stay on the platform you found them, transition them to being friends, customers, strategic partners, affiliate partners, etc. Invite them out for coffee, lunch or dinner to connect in person. As you are connecting, please make sure that private or business conversations aren't held in public. Have these conversations via messaging features, phone, email or video chat.

For the most part these platforms work the same. They just use different lingo or terminology. For example, on LinkedIn it's a connection, while on Facebook it's a friend and Twitter and Instagram use the term followers. Below are a few networking strategies that work across all platforms.

❑ Brand your profile: Remember you teach people who you are. Help them to remember you by consistently branding your profiles across each platform. Be sure that it's engaging, catches the attention of your target customer and delivers your unique value proposition.

❑ Add a professional photo that speaks to your brand and shows your personality. Please make sure that people are able to recognize you in your photo. Don't over edit your pictures. If you're 40, use a 40-year-old picture and not an 18-year-old one.

❑ Import your existing contacts from Outlook, Yahoo, Gmail, etc. and send them an invitation to connect.

❑ Reach out to friends and influencers in your industry and ask them to share your content with their audience if they found it valuable.

❑ Directly contact connections through direct mail or DM (Twitter), in-mail (LinkedIn), or via Facebook messaging to connect. After a connection is accepted, send a response to thank them for accepting. Keep in mind that many times, that these platform messaging features are inundated with sales and marketing messages, so if someone isn't familiar with you, they may not respond.

Tip: You can use Google or sites like www.emailhunter.co to search for email addresses of those that you want to connect with directly. Sign up for my 4-week networking webinar to get specific strategies and more information on how to perform these searches.

❑ Transition contacts made at events or in person to your social media platforms. Connect with them on the platforms you utilize most. Social media is like an automated follow-up and reminder system. Seeing people pop up in your feed, reminds you to follow-up with them and provides you with information to leverage. Deliver engaging content that consistently provides value and they'll reach out to you.

❑ Use keywords in your bio that speak to your brand. Keywords help your target customers find you on the various social media channels.

❑ Learn more about your connections, friends, followers, etc. by simply clicking on their names or photos and browsing their pages. While you're there, comment like and share. Share your connections events, content, posts and promotions, especially those that align with your brand, what you believe in and do. Try to do this a few times a week. In addition, don't forget to like and comment in their feed. Please note that LinkedIn does share when you have view someone's page.

❑ Engage, promote, and refer connections: Use your social media channels to engage, promote and facilitate connections. After connecting with someone, the way to get their attention is by liking, commenting, sharing and retweeting their posts. You can also periodically do "shout outs" to thank people or promote the great work they are doing. When you have two friends or connections that are involved in the same organizations, live in the same area, or that clearly should partner because their efforts are in alignment, comment on their post to see if they know each other. If they don't know each other, introduce them and tell them that you think they should meet. Inbox each of them why you think they should connect. Be excited about the introduction and tell each of them a few good things about the other.

❑ Join LinkedIn and Facebook groups, participate and consistently interact with members. Start by clicking on Groups You May Like. Join groups that are specific to your industry, career experiences and groups where your target customers are. Watch for posts and make comments. This is your opportunity to share your expertise. This will help you gain more notoriety in your field. This is also a great way to get others to notice you, make new connections and grow your network. You can even start a discussion and operate as a facilitator in the feed.

❑ Invite your connections to join groups and attend events that you think might be beneficial for them. To keep them engaged share relevant valuable content with them. When you ask a question, please don't forget to follow the feed, interact, like and respond to comments made.

❑ Create Your Own Group on Facebook and LinkedIn: Remember to use this group to further enhance your brand, so name the group accordingly. Make sure that you are posting valuable content, not just selling things in this group. Post a minimum of once a day. You must ask questions and request feedback. Remember engagement is the key.

❑ Add your main social media profile links to your email signature in the form of icons that link off to your pages to encourage everyone you correspond with to connect with you.

❑ Engage your connections by soliciting their opinions on trending topics. Use hashtag searches to find those already having these conversations and engage them on their feeds.

❑ At the event, have your followers, connections, friends, etc. post, share and pin pictures of themselves with your product or at your event. Purchase a large personalized, social media cutout frame prop and have your attendees take pictures with it at your event and post the picture using your hashtag. Have them do funny things, tag others, share a testimonial etc. You can also have a contest and give something away to the person with the funniest picture or most likes, etc.

❑ Use hashtags often as they are great for searches and can lead to more exposure. There are many people who run specific hashtag searches daily and will connect with you and retweet your content if they find value. Download the app Tags for Likes for popular hashtag ideas. Use as many or as few hashtags as you'd like to connect with your target audience and attract future followers. If you promote a resource, are at a restaurant or are wearing a major brand, tag them in a picture and using their latest hashtag.

❑ Host a recurring Follow Friday, where you encourage your network to connect with each other, share their websites, promotions and events. You could even encourage your network to refer (tag) a business they love and frequent. Switch the theme up periodically.

❑ Host a social media contest to engage your network and grad their attention.

Career Seekers:

❑ Post on your social media channels and send out a quick text letting your network know that you're on a career search and you need their help. Let them know specifically what you're looking for. Be open as opportunities present themselves, small opportunities can open big doors.

Note: Please keep in mind that employers often search your social media platforms, so be mindful of who you're connecting with as they could be seen as a reflection of you. You also want to be mindful of what you post; many people have lost opportunities as a result of posting the wrong thing.

(9) Editorials, E-books, Newspapers, Whitepapers, Business Journals or Magazines are a great resource for finding people to connect with. These documents are normally available online and in print. Search these documents to find connections. Connect with advertisers, article writers, those who are being recognized for specific accomplishments. For example, newspapers like your local Business Journal will list new businesses and congratulatory announcements when top level executives accept new positions. They also run Best of lists, Top 100 lists and award winners from local events, all great lead and connection opportunities. Send a handwritten note to congratulate an awards recipient or someone moving into a new space. You can also stop by their new location with a small welcome gift. If you publish any of the documents listed above, offer them on your website to collect email addresses.

(10) Emails and E-newsletters are a great way to initiate a connection and keep connections engaged. Make sure that you create intriguing, attention grabbing emails with great subject lines. You should always work to provide valuable content and resources. Make sure that you have permission when adding people to your email marketing lists. I would suggest that you use email marketing software to better track engagement, open and click through rates. Use various calls to action throughout your emails and e-newsletters to engage your network. Make sure that they are not all sales focused.

- www.constantcontact.com
- www.mailchimp.com

(11) Facebook: www.facebook.com

❏ Set your privacy settings accordingly. There are a number of people today, using an alias on Facebook or other social media platforms because they don't want their professional contacts or employers to find them and connect with them on their "personal" platforms. I believe that who you are is who you are and if you need to hide things from certain people, maybe you shouldn't be posting it. If you are really interested in networking and being found online, make sure that you use a consistent name and make your privacy settings public. If you tend to over share or want to limit the access of certain people, you can create specific groups on Facebook and set your privacy settings specifically for each group to control what they can and can't see.

❏ Do a Facebook Live video feed at least once a week on a topic in your area of expertise. You can also "go live" at an event you're hosting or attending.

❏ Say Happy Birthday: Facebook sends you a birthday notification on your friend's birthday. Post a fun Facebook Live happy birthday video, if you have time. If not, a simple happy birthday message or image will do. Invite them to stop by your office to pick up a birthday gift.

❏ Create a happy hour or networking event on Facebook. Invite your entire network to attend by adding them to the event. Post and comment leading up to the event to generate excitement and get your network engaged. You can also host online networking events via your social media platforms.

(12) Google: The Internet allows you access to so much information. It's one of the easiest way to gather names and contact information of those that fit your target market. You should also check out Google Plus at www.plus.google.com. If you use Gmail, check out www.clearbit.com. This Google extension allows you to pull full data profiles on those that are in your inbox.

(13) LinkedIn: www.linkedin.com

LinkedIn is a great way for business owners to not only find customers but strategic partners, employees and contract laborers. It's an amazing professional research tool and resource.

❏ Let your personality and brand shine: Don't use the automated LinkedIn connection message. Be creative and add your own special touch to every connection message. If connecting with a prospect, take a moment to view their profile to see if you are able to find a commonality or something to connect with them on and use it.

❏ Export your LinkedIn contacts into a CSV file or Excel spreadsheet, organize them alphabetically by title, city or state, etc. Use the method that works best for you to sort the list and identify your target customer. Review each connection and assign them a priority letter or number, it's totally up to you. High priority contacts can be labeled 1 or A, and the lowest priority being a 3 or C. Contact all of the 1 or A level contacts first. You may also want to start with those you have the strongest relationships first. This isn't a one-time process. I suggest that you do this at least every quarter.

❑ Position and company change notifications: LinkedIn notifies you when a connection changes company or position. Congratulate them and when they respond, let them know that you would like to do coffee or lunch to celebrate after they get settled.

Career Seekers:

❑ Research your network, type in your industry or company of interest and see what job titles exist there. There are so many creative titles in today's marketplace. Who knows you may find an area or career of interest that you never even knew existed. You can also simply run random keyword searches to see what you come up with.

❑ Find connections at a company before applying for a position, using the company search feature to search for the company by name. Search to see who you know in your network that is employed there or if they are connected to someone else that is. Reach out to them to see if you can use them as a reference and place their name in the referral box where the company asks how you heard about them. Click the words see all to view all connections that you have in a specific company. Contact the person via in mail, email or pick up the phone and give them a call. Calling them is your best bet because it allows you to discuss your qualifications and gives them an opportunity to further connect with you. If you get an interview, you can also ask them if it's okay for you to use their name.

(14) Instagram: www.instagram.com

❑ Did you know that you can direct message someone on Instagram? To use Instagram Direct, simply click the square 3D box in the upper right hand corner of the app on the home page. You can send private pictures and videos to those that you wish to connect with.

❏ Go to your profile page and click on the screen where you see followers and the number at the very top of the app. Review your list and contact those that interest you via Instagram Direct, commenting on their post or tagging them in your post.

❏ Connect your Twitter, Facebook, Swarm and Tumblr accounts to your Instagram account to post a single post across multiple channels. This could ultimately lead those that are connected with you on other channels back to your Instagram channel to connect.

(15) Pinterest: www.pinterest.com

❏ Post images with description information, and pricing that link off to products, services and programs that are on your website. Post these items to engage and grab the attention of existing and potential followers and customers.

❏ Categorize and organize your boards; add keyword descriptions to your boards to make them easier to find and to increase engagement.

❏ Add a pin button or social media icons to your blogs and website to increase followers and make it easier for others to share your content.

(16) Radio and Podcasts: Many believe that radio is a dying breed because of the advancement of video and technology as a whole. The truth is, most people aren't always in a position to sit still and watch a video, so radio is still relevant. Host a radio show or podcast. You can use your radio show or podcast to interview people from different backgrounds. Interviews are a great way to network and connect with someone. It's an amazing way to find out more about someone and their business. It's also a great way to create content for your network and keep them engaged. Use www.fiverr.com to purchase a professional into and outro for your show to further promote your brand. Include your unique value proposition. Share these shows and interviews with your network. Use these platforms to create, engage and offer your network valuable content.

(17) Twitter: www.twitter.com

❏ Set up segmented lists (customers, strategic partners, prospects, media, competitors, etc.) and check them regularly to engage those in these lists. It's also a great way to monitor what's trending in specific areas or industries.

❏ Include a click to tweet link in your emails, so that people can just click once to share the tweet with their networks. Visit www.clicktotweet.com to set it up.

❏ Host a twitter party. This is a great way to network and promote a new program, event, product or service. Identify a catchy, but short hashtag that participants can use to find you on twitter and participate in the party. You can have a special guest, do a Q and A and even do a giveaway of your new product, service or program during the party. The whole point is to engage your network around a specific topic or theme.

❏ Use www.followerwonk.com to search bios, find target market connections, compare twitter accounts, and sort followers by location, etc. You should also consider using www.twitterfeed.com and www.muckrack.com.

❏ Connect with and follow media contacts to pitch story ideas. Send a direct message to media contacts and share your ideas. Once the story is released, tag those in your network who may find it of interest.

NETWORKING VIA VIDEO

Host your own live, online networking events where multiple people can interact via Google Hangout or Skype. You can also host webinars

or record fun live videos to engage your connections. Most of the platforms offer live, real time interaction with viewers. Talk to them as you deliver valuable content, ask questions and respond when they answer. Invite your network to participate in your videos. All of these platforms also have apps that you can download to your Android or IPhone. Post, pin, tweet and share your videos on each of the social media platforms. Include a specific call to action in each video that engages your network. You can also
network with those that comment in your video feeds. Check out the following video platforms.

(18) Blab: www.blab.im

(19) Facebook Live: www.facebook.com

(20) Google Hangout: www.hangouts.google.com

(21) Periscope: www.periscope.com

(22) Skype: www.skype.com

(23) Vimeo: www.vimeo.com

(24) YouTube: www.youtube.com

(25) Websites or Blogs: Create networking opportunities via your blog or website. It's an inexpensive way to connect with and engage your audience. Add forums, live chat apps, call to action pop-ups, email sign-up apps and social media icons that are linked to your profiles. These web features give you an opportunity to further connect with those that see value in what you provide. Be a guest blogger to connect with and gain access to other bloggers followers.

(26) REFERRALS AND INTRODUCTIONS

Referrals and introductions are a major part of effective networking. If you believe in what you do and the value you provide, be bold and ask those you know for referrals, specifically those that have experienced your products and services. The best time to ask a customer for a referral is after you have closed a sale because they are excited about their new purchase. Anytime you request a referral, give them specific details about the type of person you are looking to be introduced to. Every time someone refers you, they are saying, we honor and value you and what you do. Honor them and reward those referrals that turn into business. Don't be greedy, share with those that help you get to where you want to go.

Tip: When asking for a referral be specific. For example, if you're a company in the disaster clean-up business. Don't just ask, "Do you know anyone that needs my services?" Ask, "Do you know anyone whose home has water, flood or hail damage as a result of the recent tornado or flood. We want to keep them from the added stress of dealing with insurance adjusters. All we need is the name of their insurance provider and we do the rest. Because of our relationship with insurance companies we normally have an approval and a crew on site within 3 to 4 hours of submitting your claim. Always communicate the value and results that you provide. When a referral is provided, you can jot down their information on a branded referral card or have them send an email introducing you. You can also search their contacts on LinkedIn or Facebook, so that you can ask to be connected to specific people by name.

<u>Business Owners & Professionals</u> can increase referrals by...

❑ Connect with companies that are going out of business. If you know someone in your industry that is closing their doors, ask if they are looking for someone to refer business or if you can purchase their book of business. You can also ask them if they will be keeping their phone number. If they aren't, you may be able to have it transferred into your name. Do this to get their inbound call traffic. Many times a company's contact information floats around on the web for years before it is removed.

❏ Have your clients add your contact information to their cell phone. People who don't have your contact information handy are less likely to refer you.

❏ Set up a referral rewards programs to thank your customers, family and friends for referring business. Yes, you should reward your family as well. Email your existing customers, clients and friends, describing the type of clients you have the best products and services for. Use a call to action to ask the person receiving the email to forward it to friends they want to refer. Make the referral super easy for them.

❏ Invite strategic partners to meet-up for referral lunches, where you share leads. Decide how often you will meet and where you'll meet. Encourage each person to invite a guest every month to organically grow the group. Establish guidelines to avoid opportunities for confusion.

❏ Host your own networking event or happy hour and again invite your network, encouraging them to bring others. Use the tools provided through this book to promote your event. Because you know everyone in the room, facilitate introductions to provide value and for those who bring guests, carve out time in your event for everyone to introduce themselves and their guest.

❏ Develop a referral kit. Make sure your kit has information in it that makes it easier for others to refer your business. Include "referred by" cards, a product/ service list, business cards, promo items or anything else you think might make it easier for others to send more referrals your way. Make sure it's available in pdf format.

❏ Write hand written thank you notes to express your appreciation for referrals. Be sure to show gratitude for both successful and unsuccessful referrals. When there is no sale and they don't hear anything from you there's a good chance they won't be sending any more leads your way. Even if all you send is an email, send something to say thank you.

(27) Reviews, Testimonials and Recommendations are a great networking tool. Having a number of quality business reviews/testimonials on Google, Yahoo listings, LinkedIn and Yelp can play a huge role in whether or not someone contacts you or sees you as credible. Reach out to customers after a favorable experience and ask for a testimonial or review. Send them a link with clear instructions on how to do this. Engage those that leave ratings and testimonials on the review site. Comment when applicable to say thank you. Offer them something complimentary when possible.

EVENTS AND MEET-UP GROUPS

Now, ask yourself,

❑ Where do my target customers hang out?

❑ What places do they frequent? These are the places you need to be, so that you can gain access to your customers.

❑ Where are the people that can afford my products and services?

❑ What's missing from my existing network?

❑ Who or what type of people and from what industry do I need to add to my network?

❑ Where are they?

Search various event sites and apps to find events in your area. To find their membership or attendance policies; run a Google search for the specific chamber, group or association type and your city and state to pull up their websites. Events offer great opportunities to network and market your business. Anytime there's an opportunity to attend a local community event, you or another company representative should be there. Don't forget to invite current customers and prospects to attend events that you will be attending. If there is a cost for the event, purchase their ticket, especially when it's industry specific and can add value to them.

 **Tip:** Invite a friend to come network with you and you both work the room together, introduce each other to everyone you meet. You'll cover more ground this way. Two are better than one.

BONUS: STRATEGIC SPONSORSHIPS

Most events offer you an opportunity to sponsorship or be a vendor. Most times you have the option to sponsor a table, be a title or an event or sponsor. Whatever you choose, be strategic...

❑ If you are an event or title sponsor, ask to receive a list of registered attendees, before and then a list of actual attendees after the event with contact info, so that you can follow-up with them or email them a special offer. Be sure to follow-up because that's where the magic happens. You can use the list before the event to identify people that you would like to connect with at the event. Ask the host to facilitate connections or arrange strategic seating.

❑ If you purchased a table or were given a certain number of seats or tickets as a sponsor, do not just invite all staff to occupy those seats, again be strategic. If it's a huge event, you may want to buy additional seats to have enough staff working the event. If you are a title or event sponsor, allocate three tickets for staff and give the rest to prospects. Ask the event hosts to extend the invitation to prospects that fit your target customer profile, if they have a relationship with them and you don't. Whoever owns the relationship should invite the prospect. If your table seats 10, strategically sit staff amongst prospects. You may also want to purchase additional tickets so that you can invite your top clients, add value by helping them expand their network. It's also wise to strategically mix them amongst your prospects. There is nothing better than a real life testimonial.

❏ Don't allow staff to attend and just sit at the sponsored table. Bring your most energetic and outgoing staff, have them work the room. If you are a title sponsor at an event, have your staff assist with registration, greeting and serving guests alongside event hosts. Make your team apart of the event. This is another way for attendees to experience your brand.

❏ Deliver your brand experience. Have business cards, promotional items and marketing materials available.

Be strategic, don't waste your sponsorship!

(28) Associations & Professional Groups: This includes, but not limited to realtors, plumbers, human resources, marketing, teachers, technology, engineers, etc. If either of these are in your target market, you can connect with various industry professionals in one room, by connecting with these groups and associations.

(29) Business Expos & Tradeshows: There are also tons of other expo and trade shows other there. Run a Google search for the type of expos your looking for with the year, your city and state of interest. (Example: Health Expos 2016 Dallas, TX or Technology Expo 2017 Florida). Find events at www.expodatabase.com and www.tsnn.com.

(30) Chambers of Commerce: Google Chamber of Commerce with your city and state. Chose the Chamber that represents and serves your target customer. Contact the Chamber in your area to ask questions about the demographics and engagement of their membership. These organizations host a number of networking events and meetings throughout the year that give you an opportunity to meet other business owners and professionals in the area. Most Chambers provide you with a contact list that you can use to connect with attendees after the event. They also have their full membership directory, often with contact names online. Use this directory to search for businesses by zip code, name, or industry.

(31) Conferences, Seminars, Tele-seminars and Webinars are a great way to generate leads and provide your network with valuable content. Host or attend these events to grow your network. When you attend online events, use the chat feature to connect and engage with participants. Host an event to expand and stay connected to your existing network. When people register for the event you get their contact information, so that you can follow-up and connect with them afterwards. Remember to promote your events on your social media channels and set up an event page on Facebook. Engage attendees leading up to the event. Make sure that you are providing great content that's interesting and valuable. Use the video platforms from page 93 to host an online training. You can also use www.freeconferencecall.com. Can't afford to attend an event, find ways to access attendees by being in close proximity of the event. If the event is being held at a hotel, hang out at the bar, eat a meal and have drinks there or hang out in the lobby, working. The attendees are bound to be in these high traffic areas in between sessions or after the event ends. Host a teleseminar using www.freconferencecall.com.

 **TIP:** Contact a local restaurant, coffee house, sandwich shop, or a hotel with low foot traffic about using their space at no cost. Many times they are happy to let you use it because

of the traffic you will bring. Most restaurants are free to use if your attendees purchase food and drinks. Make your attendees aware of the food/ drink minimums. You can also have the restaurant create a simple menu with 3 to 5 items on it that are within a certain price range. Be bold and make the ask. Never be afraid of no.

Other venues with low cost options to consider...

- Churches
- Hotels and convention centers
- Local co-working spaces
- Libraries
- Recreation and community centers
- www.cvent.com

(32) Cross Promotional Events: Throwing a special event just for your clients can be overwhelming and expensive. To ease the burden and get more leads, team up with another local business for a cross-promotional event. Have every business that's involved invite their own clients. Connect with businesses that compliment yours for more strategic opportunities. During the event deliver an experience that engages existing and prospective customers.

(33) Gender Specific, Political and Need Specific Events and Groups: You name it and there's a networking group for it. Google events in your area and join groups on LinkedIn and Facebook.

(34) Master Mind Groups: Start or join a group to hold each other accountable to goals, to leverage each participant's network while sharing your expertise and ideas. Meet regularly to keep each other encouraged and accountable.

(35) Ministry or Spiritual Events and Groups: There are a ton of these groups and events out there. Run a Google search to find them in your area. (Example: Meditation Events 2018 New York, NY or Women's Conference 2017 Little Rock, Arkansas)

(36) Places You Frequently Visit: Use your hobbies as networking opportunities. Network before or after a basketball game, at the art gallery or museum, or hanging out with your knitting club, etc. Don't make the mistake of overlooking the value of networking in a relaxed non-professional environment with people who have common interests, it's invaluable. Remember it all starts with a smile and hello. When at the gym, please don't disturb others while they are working out and when at church, don't disrupt service. As you network always respect the environment. Remember, the goal is to make a connection. After a connection has been made, you can work to build a relationship outside of the venue over coffee or lunch. You never know who you'll meet, if you expand your new networking limits.

- Anywhere there are kids and pets
- Doctor's office or hospital waiting room
- Golf club
- Gyms and Sporting Events
- HOA, crime watch, and neighborhood block parties
- In transit: on the bus, airplane, shuttle or train
- The Mall/ shopping centers/ grocery stores
- Political campaigns/ offices

- School, PTA meetings, Toastmasters, etc.

(37) Ribbon Cuttings & Grand Openings: These events offer you an opportunity to connect with decision makers and top leaders in a company. The energy is high so people are more open to connecting. They'll appreciate your support, thus opening the doors for a true connection. Check your local Chamber website each week for these free networking opportunities.

(38) Speed Networking Events: These fast paced events are a blast, offering you networking with a twist. Google speed networking with your city and state to find events in your area.

Websites and Apps for Networking Event Searches:

- www.allconferences.com
- www.craigslist.com
- www.eventbrite.com
- www.eventful.com
- www.facebook.com
- www.lanyrd.com
- www.meetup.com
- www.netparty.com
- www.networkafterwork.com
- www.vite.io
- www.yelp.com

TIP: There are a ton of local event sites in your area. Run a Google search, using the terms events with your city and state. To get more specific add month, date and/ or year.

(39) Volunteer Opportunities and Internships are an amazing way to meet people. Volunteer in areas that will enhance your gifts, skills, strengths and talents.

Business Owners & Professionals: Find opportunities not only where you will enjoy serving and where your target customers are.

Career Seekers: Volunteer opportunities and internships are a great was to gain experience. Be strategic and identify opportunities that will help to grow and improve your resume.

(40) Canvassing and Door-to-Door: If you're what I like to call "old school you know a little something about this. Be respectful of no soliciting signs and if you want to distribute flyers or postcards, don't forget to contact city offices to get the proper permits. No soliciting doesn't mean you can't go in and say hi. Connect with the receptionist or owner while you're there to find out more about their business products and services. You can also visit apartment complexes and other communities with a leasing office to connect with staff in an effort to identify opportunities to have a booth at a complex open house or event. If you decide to use flyers, you can hire high school or college students to help with this effort. This is a great networking platform for business owners, sales professionals and those in politics to connect with the local community.

(41) Cold Calls: It's the networking tool that most people hate, but it's very beneficial. What's the worst that could happen? All they can say is no, not interested and in that case, just move on to the next one. Focus on getting a yes, not the possibility of no. And don't forget you're only five connections away from the people you want to meet. Find out who those five people are and network your way to the people you need to connect with. Also remember to warm up the call using information found on their social media channels. For example, ask about an event or project they're working on.

TIP: Find contact info or an email online for those that you want to connect with. First identify the company's domain name, then run a search for @domainname.com to determine their email format, whether its first name or first initial, last name, etc.

To ensure social media success, planning is necessary. Below are a few ideas of content that you can use on your social media channels to engage your existing network and grab the attention of prospective connections.

(1) Record a how to video or write a how to blog with fun, step by step pictures of how to do what you're describing. Select something fun or in your area of expertise. You could even offer a different perspective than what's traditionally given.

(2) Share customer testimonials, recommendations and endorsements via video or text.

(3) Survey or poll your friends, connections and followers in relation to the services you provide, your industry, their needs, etc. Create an infographic and share the results. Facebook and twitter have great polling platforms. Ask for your audience's opinions and ideas. People love to speak their mind.

(4) Share your own content.

❑ A chapter from a book that you have written

❑ Snippets from workshops or webinars that you host

❑ A PowerPoint presentation, articles, interviews and podcasts

(5) Jump on trending topics and tie them back to your area of expertise. Use the following as resources to identify trends.

❑ Go to www.facebook.com. Trends are listed on the right-hand side of the page, underneath your event and birthday notifications. In the

Facebook app, click in the search box and scroll down past suggested searches, then it's underneath posts you may have missed.

❏ Go to www.fre.sh. This site is powered by BuzzFeed. It provides you with the fastest trending stories daily on the web.

❏ Go to www.google.com/trends/hottrends to access daily trending Google searches.

❏ Go to www.twitter.com. Trends are listed on the left side of your screen, based on your last selected location or the location near you. You can change your location at any time. In the twitter app, you can click on the search icon at the top of the app when you open it.

(6) Find a trending video, blog or article that has been shared a ton or has a huge following and agree or disagree with it. If you do this make sure you know what you're talking about. You can also debunk myths in your industry.

(7) Post fun pictures that invite your audience into your life and business. Host a caption contest. Have your network compete to write the best caption for the photo and the one with the most likes or shares wins. You can also post animated pictures (GIF files), www,giphy.com is a great GIF search tool.
(8) Don't forget to periodically share product and service promotions. Always look for ways to strategically position products and services around the content you share.

(9) Interview experts in your field and share. Start a podcast and interview exciting content creators.

(10) Share your thoughts on issues close to your heart.

(11) Host a contest or giveaway. Give away money, books, gift cards, etc.

(12) Have a little fun, play would you rather with your social media connections. Google would you rather questions or download a would you rather app for question ideas.

(13) Post and share existing content, articles, news stories, memes, scriptures, etc. Use www.storify.com to organize your social media content. Check out these additional resources.

- ❏ www.brainyquotes.com

- ❏ www.goodreads.com

- ❏ www.memegenerator.net

(14) Everybody loves product, service or resource reviews. Post reviews of your favorite things or like Oprah create a list of your favorite life, business or relationship resources, depending on your business or area of expertise.

(15) When a fun or weird national holiday comes up, share something fun that correlates with your brand. This is also a great opportunity to run a promotion. Add these holidays to your marketing calendar.

- ❏ www.holidayinsights.com/moreholidays/

- ❏ www.timeanddate.com/holidays/fun/

- ❏ Download the Bizarre Holiday app in the ITunes store.

(16) Share content or run a promotion on National Health days or months. Add these holidays to your marketing calendar.

- www.healthfinder.gov/nho/

- www.cdc.gov/women/observances/

- www.daysoftheyear.com

(17) Celebrate and share content around national holidays. Visit http://www.timeanddate.com/holidays/us/ to view national U.S. holidays.

(18) During a webinar, event or conference have members

(19) Take group photos or photos with others and share them on your social media channels, tag people that are in them and their friends will also see them. You can also do the same with videos; record a snippet of a speaker or an event and tag people that you met at the event or those that were in attendance.

TIP: Always engage your audience when they comment on your posts. Like their comments and reply periodically. Don't be anti-social in your own posts. Use calls to action in every post and always thank those that share your posts.

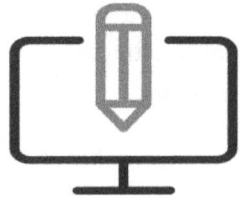

CONTENT CREATION TOOLS:

You don't have to use them all. Pick your favorites and create!

- www.canva.com: Create flyers, postcards, FB covers, etc.
- www.evernote.com: To manage content; take notes, store research and manage a project.
- www.instapaper.com: To save, read and manage articles, videos, or anything else you find while browsing the Internet.
- www.freepik.com, www.flaticon.com, www.unsplash.com and www.pixabay.com: Great resources for free images.
- www.gimp.org or www.pixlr.com: Free image editors, similar to Photoshop.
- www.google.com: To gather information and ideas.
- www.grammarly.com or correctica.com: Spell check programs - identify errors and usage issues.
- www.helpareporter.com: Identify the stories that journalists really want. Join their email list.
- www.hubspot.com and www.mashable.com: Sign up for their email lists to receive amazing tools and resources.
- www.issuu.com: Create online magazines and books.
- www.lunapic.com: A free online picture editor.
- www.portent.com/tools/title-maker: Generate content titles.
- www.quora.com: Find the answers you need and content ideas for every subject.

YOUR WEEKLY NETWORKING STRATEGY

NETWORKING STRATEGY   **Week of:** _____

Before developing a networking strategy, be sure that you are clear on the following.

(1) S.M.A.R.T. goals for your life and business. Break them down into, monthly, weekly and daily goals and tasks.

(2) Based on your goals, what resources will you need to accomplish them?

(3) Research your network and connections. What already exists within your network? Who has access to what you need?

(4) How will you access or obtain it? What's your outreach strategy? If you can't identify anyone within your network who has access to what you need, use the Six Degrees of Separation Theory. Identify the person who has what you need and then the five people between you and them.

FOLLOW YOUR INTERNAL GPS

Practice mindfulness, listening for direction as you move through your day. Take a couple of 10 to 15-minute breaks in your day, where you simply sit still, upright, eyes closed, clearing your mind. Each day as you rise and move throughout your day, you must learn to follow your internal GPS. Pay attention to names you come across when you're cleaning up. Themes or subjects that show up repeatedly. Follow the signs. I also encourage you to reach out to people that cross your mind or that randomly pop up somehow. Stop writing things off as coincidence. God is always speaking, and life is always pointing you in the direction you should go, if you would only pay attention.

Let's break the plan down into bite-sized pieces.

ESTABLISH WEEKLY GOALS

Review and identify your business and personal goals and needs for the week. Start with the big overwhelming stuff, then work your way down to the smaller tasks. Remember, the longer you put it off, the harder it becomes. Start your day pursuing and overtaking.

- What are your goals this week – sales, marketing, activity, etc.?

- What resources do you need this week – money, people, tools, etc.? List everything you need to accomplish your goals.

STRATEGIC CONNECTIONS

- Who do you need or will you plan to meet this week? Again these connections are based on your goals and needs.

- Be specific, make a list of 5 to 10 names. Select a number based on your capacity and workload. What can you manage this week? After you have your list of names, search LinkedIn to identify your other five degrees of separation.

- Will these connections be made via phone, in person or online?

- What's your plan, your reason for contacting them? Are they a prospective or existing customer, friend, strategic partner or affiliate? If needed, devise a script to make these calls a little less intimidating.

☐ Identify the date and time of contact. Schedule it as an appointment on your calendar?

☐ Who do I need to reconnect with this week? Look 6 months out. Do you have events coming up that you will need resources for? Make these connections now.

ENGAGE SOCIAL MEDIA CONTACTS

Schedule time each day to strategically manage your social media accounts. Allocate time for planning, connecting, posting, commenting each day to engage new and existing connections. Schedule small blocks of time in the morning, lunch and in the evening to check and manage your account. I usually check my accounts at 7:30 AM, Noon and 6:30 PM. I spend about 10 to 15 minutes during each allocated time period. I do all of my planning and prescheduled posts on Sunday.

❑ Search contacts, by city, state, industry, other key words, etc.

❑ Select a minimum of 10 new social media contacts to connect with this week (two a day). Comment on posts and engage them on the platform of your choice.

❑ Identify social media contacts that you can meet with in person?

Social media management requires a lot of time. If you can afford to hire a social media manager do so.

CLIENT & PROSPECT CELEBRATIONS

Check calendars, CRM and social media channels for birthdays, anniversaries, marriages, awards ceremonies and recognitions. Send hand written notes or cards. Schedule a recurring reminder on your phone to check first thing in the morning each day. You may want to check on the first of the month through the first week of the following month. If you are planning to mail something, you will need to at least plan two weeks out. Emails, posts, video messages and texts can be sent the day of.

EVENTS TO ATTEND THIS WEEK

Add events you plan to attend this week to your calendar, include event name, date, time and location. Use the websites listed on pages 102 - 103 to identify events you are interested in attending. Don't forget to schedule a reminder to share the event on your social media channels (tag contacts) and email an invitation to specific people you want to connect or reconnect with. Look for events a month ahead and add them to your calendar, so that you will have ample time to invite guests.

CONNECTIONS TO FACILITATE THIS WEEK

Be a strategic connector. Identify two to five people within your network that you can strategically connect. These people would undoubtedly add value to each other's lives or businesses. Connect people in your network. Send notes of introduction via email or direct message, making them aware of why you're connecting them and the value you see that they could provide to each other. You can even tag connections in a comment or post.

WEEKLY RESULTS

Reflect on and celebrate your accomplishments this week!

❏ How many contacts did you make this week?

❏ How many connections or responses did you receive?

❏ Number of clients retained? Revenue retained? You must be just as mindful of retention efforts as you are recruitment efforts. Remember, it costs more to bring on a new customer than it does to retain and existing one.

❏ New clients acquired? Additional revenue generated as a result? Write down the names of every new client in your notebook or journal, focus on each name. Remember, these are people, not just revenue or numbers. Send a welcome email or thank you card. Thanking them for doing business with you.

WEEKLY REVIEW

- Hot leads and prospective opportunities generated?

- What areas or activities did you struggle with this week? Do you need training or coaching? Reflect on what happened. How can you do better next week.

- Identify areas of need or lack. How can you meet the need or fill the gaps?

- What worked well this week?

- What can be improved? What changes do you need to make? What can you try next week?

- Research strategies that work; take what fits your audience, personality and strategy, then implement it.

Each week answer the strategy questions to help you establish strategic networking goals, like how many events to attend, how often, who to connect with, etc. After you have identified your action items, you must schedule them. Add them to your calendar, set reminder alarms and color code them if needed to ensure that you get them done.

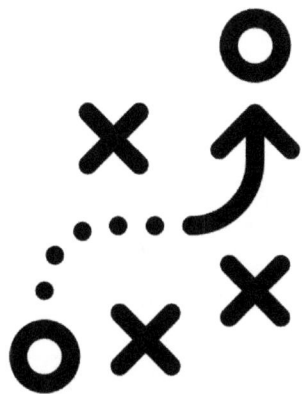

DURING THE EVENT

- ❏ BE You, DO You and HAVE Fun Doing It!
- ❏ A Networkers Daily Prayer
- ❏ Strategies for Effective Networking
- ❏ Strategies for Delivering Your Award Winning Pitch
- ❏ Graceful Exit Strategies

"Be persistent, be persistent, they say. But please, do not mistake being a pest for being persistent."
~ Nike Thaddeus

6 BE YOU, DO YOU AND HAVE FUN DOING IT!

Do nothing out of selfish ambition or vain conceit. Rather, in humility value others above yourselves, [4] not looking to your own interests but each of you to the interests of the other.   (Philippians 2:3-4)

Networking is not about just connecting people. It's about connecting people with people, people with ideas, and people with opportunities. (Michele Jennae)

Like everything else in this world, networking has lost its authenticity. Everyone is so focused on what they can get that they miss the opportunity to receive the greater benefits of truly being connected. I can't tell you how many times, I've heard people say, "I hate networking." And when I asked why, I would get all types of reasons like, it's too hard, there are too many aggressive sales people, I don't have time, it's pointless or it's a waste of time.

Every time I train business groups, I always ask how many of you have a bag or drawer filled with business cards at your home or office?

It never fails over half of the room usually raises their hands.
When I ask, how many of you have contacted or followed up with these leads, over 80% of their hands go down. We have to do better. There could literally be money, strategic partners, customers and resources in that drawer or bag. We have to stop making networking hard because no matter what your reason for hating networking is, we all need networking in our businesses, lives and careers to achieve success. You have to take ownership of the fact that you were created to interact with others, to exchange services, resources and information, while cultivating productive relationships. The truth is, most people hate networking because of the fears they have surrounding it, the fear of rejection, the fear of stepping outside of their comfort zone to speak to someone or the fear of failure. I know it sounds crazy, but even the fear of what would happen if you actually got the deal or made the sale is just as crippling and often times what keeps us from accessing all that we have been predestined for. It's time for you to release the fear that's keeping you stuck. It's time for you to step outside of your comfort zone and access what's rightfully yours. The only way to do this is to live in the present, allowing things to JUST BE!

> **The only networking rule you need to follow to maximize your results is BE You, DO You and HAVE FUN DOING IT!**

As you network, be yourself and share your gifts with the world, forget about all the what if's and networking rules. The rules are just another distraction, prolonging your date with destiny. With anything you learn, use what fits with who you are, your personality and what you are called to do. Everything doesn't work for everybody. What made one person successful, may not work for the next, so do you! So where do you start?

It's absolutely up to you. As you network, focus on being conscious and aware, listening to your internal GPS, so that you don't miss any opportunities; it will never steer you wrong. Smile and greet every person you pass. Ultimately, just be good to people, always ready to give and serve. Don't be so focused on the intended outcome that you miss your true assignment and the real opportunities being made available to you. Just be authentic and allow everything to flow authentically. Become mindful of and live in the flow, awake, consciously aware of everything going on in and around you, allowing everything to happen naturally as you walk in love. What does this mean? Love is action, so seek to perform the necessary actions each day that love requires and allow love to orchestrate the intended outcome. This could be practicing patience, kindness, a smile, being a listening ear, greeting someone, or offering a smile. Serve others with your gift(s), whether it's sharing your energy, encouraging them or speaking life into their dead situations. As you do this, you will see that opportunities to sell your products and services will naturally open. Life prepares and sets you up for everything that you are called to do. It also provides you with everything you need to be successful, even if it's in the

---

A NETWORKERS' DAILY PRAYER

"Lord, I thank you for opening my eyes, ears and heart to be aware of those that you have assigned me to today. Thank you for speaking clearly and audibly to me. For revealing to me, every preordained, divine connection that you have orchestrated to usher me into destiny. I thank you for ordering my steps today, so that my path will cross with whomever you have called me to connect with and serve today. Thank you for increased wisdom, knowledge and understanding as I take this journey to destiny, connecting with those you've called me to. Thank you for divine strategies as we interact and giving me exactly what to say to them and how to say it.

AMEN

form of another vessel (person). All too often when we need money, we are specifically looking for it to come in the form of a check, cash or a credit card. Because you are focused on it coming in these forms, when God sends it to you through a business opportunity or a person who could write the check or offer you a job, you miss it. The same thing holds true of needing marketing or sales assistance and meeting someone who shows you how to do it at low or no cost. There's always a ram in the bush. God always provides, usually in unconventional ways. This is why awareness is necessary. You must also be ready to act by faith. Yes, I said it, even networking requires faith. It requires that you trust that what is supposed to happen, will happen, if you are patient, submitting to God's will, listening for instruction, so that you can connect to what and who you are called to connect to at the appropriate time.

As you network, your focus should be on giving, expecting nothing in return with the caveat of, if the opportunity to make a sale presents itself, you will pursue it, unapologetically. It's absolutely okay to make a sale at a networking event, just don't be so focused on it that you miss an assignment. Don't miss the bigger picture or opportunity in your urgency to make a sale. You must learn to allow opportunities to occur in their appointed time as to not contaminate or screw them up because you weren't ready for them. When you take the time to connect, you get to listen and understand the other person's holistic needs, who they are and how to strategically serve them. You get to hear their true desires and needs beyond what is being said.

If you are at a networking event, don't focus on "working the room," meeting as many people as you can, closing sales, or running around the room, trying to collect as many cards as you can. Relax, find your flow and be open to moving as it guides you. After a while, you'll find what works for you based on your personality, gifts and goals. Move beyond titles, assumptions and judgement, let love be your guide. Shift your focus to being conscious and truly connecting. The whole point of the act of networking is to connect, so that you can hear what isn't being said and fully understand what is required to meet the other person's needs. Remember, you can only build and nurture a relationship only after a connection has been made. Set your sights on the big picture of building a mutually beneficial, productive relationship. If you came prepared to connect with a specific person start there. If you don't have a specific person you want to meet, start by connecting with the host. Greet them and tell them who you're looking to connect with. See if they have any recommendations on who you should meet or are available to help you make connections. If the host can't connect you, no worries, you've got it covered. Feel free to pursue strategic connections first, but don't waste time standing around waiting for them if they are busy. Engage others while you wait. If they end up free and you're engaged in conversation with someone else, politely excuse yourself or invite the other person to join you.

Again, there is no right or wrong way to network as long as you're being yourself. Like Nike says, JUST DO IT!

STRATEGIES FOR EFFECTIVE NETWORKING

To network effectively, you must learn to **JUST BE!**

☐ Be prepared: bring business cards and marketing materials with you. You should also have your *Award-Winning Pitch* (AWP) on standby. Based on your audience, be prepared with a *Unique Value Proposition* that speaks to them.

☐ Be on time: Don't arrive late. You don't want to miss anything.

☐ Be yourself: Be authentic and transparent: Trust, integrity and character are needed to be a referable networker. Share your energy, personality and spirit with others. You'll be more memorable as a result.

☐ Be aware, conscious and available: Go with the flow, so that you don't miss an assignment. Your agenda comes second. Listen for access cues that allow you to make connections or "make the ask," determine which is appropriate by listening intently and asking the right questions. You will find that the person in need will make and close the sale themselves. The goal of networking is not to walk out of the room having made an immediate sale, but to make connections that you can follow-up on and build productive relationships that could ultimately lead to a profitable exchange, sale or referrals.

☐ Be open and fair: Be open to meeting new people. Don't snub others because they don't qualify as your target customer. Move beyond titles and judgements. Focus on connecting. If you don't feel it, that's okay, move on. You're not going to connect with everyone. Stop running from salesmen and women. There is no need to be annoyed by their aggressiveness. They are only doing their job. Remember that the more salesmen sale, the more money businesses have to hire and pay higher salaries. If you're not interested, just say so. I promise you they won't get offended. You should consider connecting with, instead of avoiding sales professionals because they are often times the most connected people in the room.

☐ Be confident: Walk in tall, shoulders back, head held high. Give firm, confident handshakes and make eye contact. Remember you are a masterpiece, created by the God.

☐ Be fearless and proactive: Walk up to people you feel drawn to and introduce yourself.
☐ Be an experience: Be presentable, friendly and professional. Stand out, greet every person you encounter, be the light that brightens the room. Always Be Smiling! Don't forget to greet the host when you arrive and thank them before you leave. Dress accordingly and pay attention to the details of your brand.

☐ Be creative: Don't start a conversation by asking others what they do for a living. Switch it up a little. Ask them things like, who are you? What are your gifts? What are you passionate about? What do you think makes you unique? What's is the happiest day of your life to date? If it was your last day on earth and you could do one thing, what would it be? Ask them to tell you about themselves and hobbies. There are no rules. Ask them whatever you want to get them to open up.

☐ Be inclusive: Don't leave anyone standing on the sidelines. Go over to them and invite them into your conversations. No one should be left out. Ask, "Is there anyone I can introduce you to?"

☐ Be a connector: Connect Everywhere You Go!

☐ Be strategic, listen and watch for key details that are guiding the interactions and outcomes of those you connect with. Write notes on the back of their card to remember connection details that will be valuable when following up after the event. Use these details to add value. If you discuss networking strategies for Engineers, email them a pdf with your 7 Top Secret Networking Strategies for Engineers.

☐ Be respectful: Don't force yourself or your products on others. A lot of people struggle with saying no.

When people come to network, they don't want to be stuck carrying around a bunch of paper that they don't want. Before distributing marketing materials, establish interest or need. Keep in mind that these materials are your investment. Its costs money to print, so don't let it go to waste.

☐ Be online: If someone doesn't have a business card, jot down their name, number and email address or connect with them via social media on the spot. Once you connect with or friend them, screen shot an image of their profile, so you don't forget to follow-up. I don't hand out business cards unless I get the other persons contact info first because most people don't follow-up. They just collect cards.

☐ **BE CONSISTENT, FOLLOW UP AND FOLLOW-THROUGH:** The real magic happens after the event. This is when the real relationship building begins. Add your contacts to a CRM and the social media channels in which you are active.

STRATEGIES FOR DELIVERING AN AWARD-WINNING PITCH (AWP)

☐ Keep your pitch short, sweet and to the point. Don't ramble on and on. Make your pitch less than 30 seconds long. Don't use too many technical terms. No one should have to use a Webster's Dictionary or Google during your pitch.

☐ Speak clearly to your ideal customer. Speak their language at industry specific events and address their needs and concerns to show your level of expertise. At generic networking events, don't use too much technical language - be mindful of your audience. It could limit your referral opportunities as others outside the industry may know someone, but not understand the jargon.

☐ Don't be boring, depressed or monotone – deliver it with fire, passion and energy. Whatever you have to do to reconnect with your passion and energy before delivering your pitch – do it. When you're done, your audience should want to know more about what you do. If you're not excited about what you do, your product or service, no one else will be.

☐ Be dramatic and expressive. Bring props, if you'd like. Let your personality shine through. Get the audience engaged and involved, during your pitch.

☐ Share the names of top clients without bragging and only if it's to make a point or give an example. Your pitch should demonstrate credibility. Let us know who you are, what you've done, who your customers are...who you do business with, especially if they are known or respected. Do this without being arrogant! For example, if your company works with a company like AT&T or a major school district, say it. If you've helped your customer attain $500,000...spread the word.

☐ Pull at the audiences' heart strings. Tell them what problems you solve. Identify the issue's your customers face, so that you can develop and deliver a pitch that will make them feel what you do. Draw on the pain that the problem you address causes or the joy it brings, make them feel like what you offer is exactly what they need. Connect with them intellectually, physically, emotionally, or spiritually. Tap into their five senses (see, hear, taste, touch, and smell).

☐ Deliver your value proposition. Tell them what makes you unique. What makes your solution special? Tell them what problem you solve and how you do it. Tell them about the results you provide to your clients.

☐ Don't sound like you're reading a script. You want to sound as natural as possible, as if you're talking to a friend. Stand in the mirror. Rehearse and practice your pitch, if you have to, but make sure you don't sound like a robot. Use vocal variances, project your voice and add a little dramatic flair. Act as if you are competing for a Grammy nomination. Use powerful, action packed, descriptive words to make your point.

☐ End with a call to action.

☐ Repeat your name and company name at the beginning and the end of your pitch.

GRACEFUL EXIT STRATEGIES

Ever meet that one person at a networking event that talks forever or wants to tell you their life story, never making a point. They are so sweet, so you don't want to be rude. We've all been there, tied up in a conversation that is going nowhere, the person is rambling on and on and it seems like the conversation will never end. Use the following strategies to break away without being rude or disrespectful.

☐ Pull out a business card, if you're interested in connecting later and with a huge smile say, "Well, I know that you came here to network, so

I'm going to let you make your rounds. (Placing your hand on their arm or shoulder) Before we go, I want to give you my card. (Reach in your pocket and grab one) Give me a call and let's connect in the coming weeks. (Extend your hand for a handshake) It was truly a pleasure meeting you."

☐ If you're not interested in following up with the person say, Steven, I could stand here talking to you forever, but I have to make a few more connections before I leave, I wanted to connect with Nancy over there (pointing in her direction). I know that there are others you want to meet as well, so I'm going to let you get to it. (Patting on them on the shoulder as you exit stage left) We've got connections to make. You have a good evening.

☐ Lisa, let's finish this conversation over coffee because well be here all night. I will give you a call to schedule time for us to meek in the coming weeks. Does Wednesday work? What's the best time for you? Great, let's make it happen. (Make sure that you exchange business cards.)

☐ If all else fails, introduce them to someone you know or met earlier. You can say, "You need to meet Kim, she is a Non-Profit Organization Coach. She can help you get your 501c3 certification fast. Let me introduce you to her. Walk him or her over to the connection, introduce them and make them aware of why you connected them. When they get going, you can touch one of them on the shoulder with a smile to get their attention and back away from the conversation.

"Do what most people won't, so you can have what most people don't" ~Itzik Amiel

AFTER THE EVENT

- ☐ The Fortune Is in the Follow-Up
- ☐ The 5 Step Networking Follow-Up Process

Success comes from taking the initiative and following up... persisting... eloquently expressing the depth of your love. What simple action could you take today to produce a new momentum toward success in your life?
~Tony Robbins

# THE FORTUNE IS IN THE
FOLLOW-UP

"Knowing is not enough; we must apply. Willing is not enough; we must do." ~ Johann Wolfgang von Goethe

The fortune is in the follow-up. After a networking event, don't get all in your head. It's easy to process how it was a waste of time or that you didn't meet anyone of value and so on and so forth. Keep in mind that not all networking events will immediately lead to a sale or feel like they were worth it. So work your connections before you jump to any conclusions and decide not to return. Remember, that every person you connected with has a network as well, so your networking doesn't stop with them. Find them on LinkedIn and explore the possibilities to encourage yourself after a failed attempt at networking. There's always something to be grateful or thankful for in every situation or circumstance. Instead of focusing on what didn't happen, find the positive, start by expressing gratitude for the opportunity to connect with new people. This is also a great opportunity to take a moment to focus on lessons learned. After each event consider the following.

☐ What went well?

- ☐ Did you make any strategic connections?

- ☐ What can you improve upon to increase your results?

- ☐ What things did you notice?

- ☐ How can you improve your value proposition or pitch?

- ☐ How can you be more strategic?

- ☐ What new questions or conversation starters can you add?

Once you've processed all of this, you can begin the real work. The real magic of relationship building is in what happens after the event. Yet for most there is no magic because people take the business cards they've collected and drop them in a drawer or they never follow-up. You should make it a point to follow-up with someone within a week of meeting them, even if all you do is send them a friend request that says, "It was truly a pleasure to meet you. Let's stay connected." Hey, something is better than nothing at all. You should especially follow-up immediately if a business opportunity was discussed. I have met numerous people that I wanted to support or buy from, only to follow-up with them and have them not respond or follow-through. Are you guilty of this? Are you missing sales because of your inconsistent follow-up? Can you identify opportunities missed because you didn't follow-up or follow-through? Many times you are your own problem because you drop the ball.

Boldness, consistency, persistence and follow-through are the keys to phenomenal follow-up.

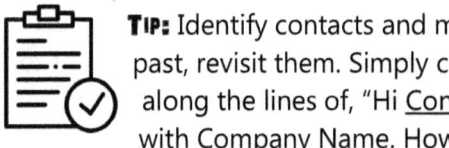

TIP: Identify contacts and missed opportunities from the past, revisit them. Simply contact them and say something along the lines of, "Hi Contact Name, this is Your Name with Company Name. How are you today? (Response) We spoke a few months ago and you were interested in purchased 10 copies of Created to Network and booking me to speak at your next women's event. I wanted to touch base with you to see if you still had women in your group who are struggling in business and would benefit from my networking strategies?

You can script this however you'd like. Do what work for you to reclaim the connection and sale.

CUSTOMER RELATIONSHIP MANAGEMENT (CRM)

So now that you've made the connection and you've collected all these business card, what do you do?

First of all, the biggest mistake that most people make is trying to manage their relationships from that drawer filled with cards, sticky notes or sheets of paper. If you don't have a *relationship management database*, implement one immediately, especially if you are an entrepreneur, sales professional or career seeker. You don't have to work for a major company to use one. Start managing your CRM while your business is small, so that as you grow, it becomes a part of the culture. A relationship management database is critical for any serious networker because it allows you to track contact information and interactions with your connections. There is no way you can remember every conversation, birthday, wedding anniversary, if someone passed or struggled with a major illness, etc. All of this information is very important because it helps strengthen your connection and relationship when people know that you care. If you don't already have a database in place, that's okay, get one. You can even export your email and LinkedIn contacts and import them into your new database. Here are a few databases to consider.

- ❏ www.hubspot.com/products/sales

- ❏ www.insightly.com

- ❏ www.lessannoyingcrm.com

- ❏ Microsoft Access

- ❏ Microsoft Excel spreadsheet

- ❏ www.zoho.com

Fields to consider, so that you are able to data sort and manage your contacts effectively, include name, address, city, state, zip code, phone, email, where you met the contact, notes and category. It is also in your best interest to be able to track contacts and interactions. You can use the notes area to put information like birthdays, anniversaries and other info that you can use to further connect with your contacts. I also recommend segmenting your customers appropriately for target marketing initiatives. Don't send everyone the same information, even if all you do is separate your contacts into two groups, prospects and customers

THE 5 STEP NETWORKING FOLLOW-UP PROCESS

After any networking event, your first priority is to sort through your contacts (cards), decide how you want to categorize them. I usually place my cards in three stacks, immediate opportunities (hot leads), prospective business opportunities (warm leads) and connections (cold leads).

Input everyone that you deem a viable lead into your CRM database, segmenting them accordingly. Remember that relationships take time to build and most times closing a sale takes numerous contacts, so you must design a process that works for you and stick to it. Make sure that your process keeps prospects engaged and connected to you until they are ready to make a purchase.

Please note that you don't have to manually type in your business cards because there are various apps available to make this process fast and easy. With technology, you can now scan your cards and sync the info to your computer or cellphone. Check out these apps for scanning and importing business cards.

- ❏ CamCard
- ❏ ScanBizCards
- ❏ CardKeeper

After adding new contacts to your CRM, send them a connection request on the social media platform(s) that you utilize regularly. I usually add all contacts that I input in my CRM to LinkedIn and Facebook because I use these two platforms the most. You have to be crazy or give off bad vibes or energy not to be added to my network. Connecting via social media provides you with access to a connections life and business like never before, thus exposing you to every opportunity available to meet their needs. Once they accept your invite, browse their timeline, post on their wall, like and comment. Social media is amazing; it serves as a reminder, touch point and follow-up system. If you don't have a CRM, this is a great resource to use until you implement one. Every time someone pops up in your feed it's a reminder to follow-up and connect with them. For example, when a connection posts about themselves or a child getting engaged, this post offers various opportunities, after you have properly congratulated them on the engagement.

Check out the opportunities available from a single post.

- Insurance Agent: Reach to them about merging their policies and getting them a better rate.
- Travel Agent: Vacation options for their honeymoon
- Real Estate Agent/ Apartment Locater: Locate them a new home to make new memories together.
- Movers: Self explanatory
- Photographer/ Videographer: Wedding pics and video.
- Chef or Caterer: Duh! They have to eat.
- Bakery: No wedding is complete without a cake.
- Organizer/ Interior Decorator: They will need to organize and merge their belongings. As well as mesh their styles.
- Counseling: Premarital and ongoing
- Life Coach: Navigating this new journey
- Attorney: Now-a-days pre-nuptial agreements are the thing to do. They may also be looking to develop a will or need other planning services.
- Jewelers: This is a given.
- Church or event rental facilities: To host their wedding.
- Uber drivers, car rental facilities or a limo company: They will need transportation for their wedding and to/ from the airport for or while on their honeymoon.

STEP 02

After you have added them on social media, send a personalized *pleasure to meet you email*. Create a generic email template in a word document or save the email in your draft or a special email folder for use on the go. You can edit this email and personalize it further as needed. Be engaging, let your personality shine in the email. Use the notes you made on the back of the card to further connect and remind them of who you are after the event, especially if the event was huge. If the person is someone that you want to further connect or do business with, make this known in your pleasure to meet you email. Let them know that you'd love to schedule some time to meet with them over coffee or lunch and include your online calendar so that they can simply select the date and time that works for them based on your availability. If you use an online calendar, please make sure that it is updated regularly. The online calendar makes scheduling events and meetings easier. If you don't have an online calendar, suggest two or three dates and times for them to choose from.

Things to include in or with your email...

❑ A resource that further connects them to your brand and shows credibility. If you spoke about something specific, this is your opportunity to provide them with more information.

❑ Social media, website and newsletter links for platforms in which you are active. Remember: never add anyone to your e-newsletter list without permission. Use social media icons in your email, instead of links; it looks more professional.

❑ If you truly connected with the person and they seem to be a good person (trust your gut), connect them with someone in your network that would be of value to them.

Career Seekers:

❑ Send a pleasure to meet you email after the event with your resume and cover letter attached that will make you stand out. Because no one mails anything anymore, mail yours and be creative. Send it in a Top Secret stamped envelope and on an extra sheet placed over your cover letter and resume, say something like, "You are receiving this top secret information before anyone else has a
chance to view it.

Make it like the top secret file of a super hero, because you are one. Use your *Purpose Brand* to grab their attention. For example, if you're an architect build your resume to resemble a blueprint or with a blue print background. If you're a music teacher, make a portion of your resume or cover letter into a song. Step outside the box of traditional resumes and cover letters. Let your personality shine.

STEP 03

Send thank you and congratulatory emails or cards. After the event if someone gave you something or facilitated a connection, thank them. Also, if you feel led to, take a moment to send a thank you card or email to the host. These are great people to be connected to. If you attended an event where someone received an award, send them a congratulatory card or email. If they are a really good lead, send a giant candy bar, a fruit basket, flowers, etc. Be creative and have a little fun with it. STAND OUT!

STEP 04

Call those you are interested in truly building a relationship with, whether that's to make a sale or establish a strategic partnership with. Do this a few days, no more than a week after the initial email was sent, if no response was received from the email you sent. If it was a strong lead, pick up the phone and call them.

STEP 05

Call again. If you have their mailing address, send a card, postcard or letter. Stay on top of prospective opportunities. I will usually follow-up one more time two weeks later, then again two weeks after that. If your prospect doesn't respond after you have contacted them three times, take a break or stop by their office and leave a $5 Starbuck gift card with a fun note. If you have connected with them via social media channels or your email distribution list, keep them engaged there. You can always try them again six months to a year later.

TIP: Add networking calls and meetings to your weekly calendar. Every time you make new contacts, follow-up with them within a week to schedule a one-on-one meeting. Make one-on-one networking meetings apart of your weekly networking strategy, especially when you meet a hot lead or possible strategic partner. Aim to have 3 to 5 one-on-one's a week Keep it simple, meet over coffee.

Remember, TAKE ACTION...JUST DO IT! There are more than enough opportunities in the world for everyone. If you can't find an opportunity create it!

SPREAD THE WORD

I need your help. If you appreciated and valued the contents of this book, help me spread the word.

How can you help?

❑ Send out a text or email, telling everyone you know about this book, encouraging them to purchase a copy. Visit my website www.createdtonetwork.com for an email or text that you can copy and paste.

❑ Purchase copies for every entrepreneur, career seeker, college graduate and sales professional you know.

❑ Post a picture of yourself with your copy of Created to Network on your social media channels. Share something you have need of and use #CreatedToNetwork.

❑ Leave a book review on amazon. You can also type up a 2 to 3 sentence testimonial and share it on social media with a picture of you holding the book, using #CreatedToNetwork.

❑ Book me to speak at your next event. Share my contact info with the speaker or event coordinator at your office, college/ university, local Chamber, or church. I speak at business events, conferences, workshops, colleges and universities.

❑ Contact me to host a Created to Network Strategy Session for your network. All you need is a meeting space. Get 25 people to attend and I'll come for free. Email admin@movebeyondmotivation.com for more details.

❏ Register for an upcoming Created to Network webinar or purchase the home study program. Learn in the comfort of your own home or office.

❏ Like me on Facebook, connect with me on LinkedIn and follow me on Periscope, Instagram and Twitter for spiritually based personal and professional development training that is designed to unlock your divine potential and lead you into destiny. My name across all channels is kishalallen. Just look for the profile picture with the giant smile.

I truly appreciate your referrals. Please make sure that those you refer mention your name and email, so that I can send you something to show my gratitude.

Email admin@movebeyondmotivation.com for speaking engagement requests or to share your thoughts, comments or ideas about this guide.

REFERENCES & RESOURCES

- ❑ Quick View: Visual Snapshots of God's Word. New International Version Bible. Grand Rapids, Michigan: Zondervan, 2012. Print.

- ❑ "Biblegateway.com: A Searchable Online Bible in Over 150 Versions and 50 Languages." Web. 11 January 2016

- ❑ "Google." Google. Web. 01 May 2016

- ❑ "U.S. and World Population Clock." Population Clock. Web. 01 May 2016

- ❑ "Famous Quotes at BrainyQuote." BrainyQuotes. Web. 07 April 2016

- ❑ "Goodreads." Goodreads. Web. 23 April 2016.

- ❑ "Dictionary and Thesaurus | Merriam-Webster." Merriam-webster.com. Web. 10 November 2016

- ❑ Strategy icon made by Gregor Cresnar from www.flaticon.com

- ❑ Notepad Icon made by Madebyoliver from ww.flaticon.com

- ❑ People icons made by Freepik from www.flaticon.com

- ❑ Computer icon made by Gregor Cresnar from www.flaticon.com

Before creating another vision board, purchase your copy of Manifesting MORE. Rome wasn't built in a day and neither should your vision.

Purchase your copy today at www.movebeyondmotivation.com.

[24] And let us consider how to stir up one another to love and good works, [25] not neglecting to meet together, as is the habit of some, but encouraging one another, and all the more as you see the Day drawing near. (Hebrews 10: 24-25)

www.ingramcontent.com/pod-product-compliance
Lightning Source LLC
Chambersburg PA
CBHW070852050426
42453CB00012B/2148